D1121276

Other Kaplan Books for College-Bound Students

The Procrastinator's Guide to the ACT*

By the Staff of Kaplan, Inc.

Simon & Schuster

NEW YORK · LONDON · SINGAPORE · SYDNEY · TORONTO

*ACT is a registered trademark of ACT, Inc., which neither sponsors nor endorses this product.

Kaplan Publishing
Published by Simon & Schuster
1230 Avenue of the Americas
New York, NY 10020

ACT is a registered trademark of ACT, Inc. The material in this book is up-to-date at the time of publication. However, ACT, Inc. may have instituted changes in the test after the book was published. Be sure to carefully read the materials you receive when you register for the test.

If there are any important late-breaking developments—or any changes or corrections to the Kaplan test preparation materials in this book—we will post that information at **kaptest.com/publishing**. Check to see if there is any information posted there regarding this book.

Contributing Editors: Seppy Basili, Trent Anderson, Dan McGrew, Justin Serrano
Project Editor: Eileen Mager
Cover Design: Cheung Tai
Production Manager: Michael Shevlin
Editorial Coordinator: Deá Alessandro
Executive Editor: Del Franz

Special thanks to Ruth Baygell.

Manufactured in the United States of America
Published simultaneously in Canada

January 2003

10 9 8 7 6 5 4 3 2 1

ISBN 0-7432-3512-6

CONTENTS

PART FIVE: The ACT Science Reasoning Test

Appendix

PREFACE

pro•cras•ti•na•tor (*n*): one who puts off intentionally the doing of something that should be done*

Hmmm… sound like anyone you know? Let's face it: We all procrastinate. It's natural to put off doing something boring, difficult, or unpleasant (such as studying for the ACT) in favor of doing something fun. And chances are, between rushing to classes, basketball games, and your part-time job, you barely have enough time these days for eating and sleeping, let alone sitting down and studying material that won't even help you pass tomorrow's biology quiz.

So now you're in a tight spot: The ACT is looming on the horizon, and, true to form, you haven't started studying yet. Wouldn't it be nice if you could use the little bits of free time you have left—the odd hour here, half-hour there—to somehow get in some solid preparation?

Well, now you can. The book you're holding in your hand is designed for the student who wants (or needs) to prepare on the run. Here you'll find just about all of the most important things

*Merriam-Webster's Collegiate® Dictionary, Tenth Edition

you need to know before walking in to these two tests. And all of this information is laid out for you in 14 easy steps, so that you can learn each step fast, move on to the next activity, and get a great score when you actually take the test.

Don't get the wrong idea: This book won't give you comprehensive test preparation. Reaching your maximum score on the ACT will take a thorough, considered effort, and Kaplan publishes other books that provide a more in-depth approach to taking these exams. But you can still benefit from having a portable companion to carry around—a pocket guide to basic skills, techniques, and strategies that will make you a better ACT test-taker.

How much of a difference can this last-minute help make? Consider this: You can boost your score just by getting a couple of extra questions correct on each section! But you won't accomplish this by getting bogged down with long vocabulary lists and reams of math principles. You *can* do it by absorbing Kaplan's targeted test-taking strategies in the following pages. Through this quick, step-by-step approach, your energies will be focused on the essential elements of the exam—places where you can really boost your score easily.

So don't panic. You might think you need 25 hours in a day to get everything done, but with *The Procrastinator's Guide to the ACT* in hand, you still have an opportunity to boost your score.

PREPARING FOR THE ACT

STEP 1:
INTRODUCTION TO THE ACT

You've probably heard rumors to the effect that the ACT is a tough exam. Well, the rumors are true. In fact, the ACT is probably one of the toughest exams you'll ever take.

Should that faze you, given that you have only a few weeks before you take the exam? No. Honestly. For one thing, if you carry out the program outlined in this book, you'll have done more preparation for the ACT than most other people sitting with you in the examination room. And since the test is marked "on a curve," your weeks of preparation will definitely put you at an advantage over your peers.

But you've got some work to do between now and then. That's why it's so important that you take the test in the right spirit. Don't be timid in the face of the ACT. Don't let it bully you. You've got to take control of the test. Our mission in this book is to show you exactly how to do that—in a few short weeks.

Here are the three things you'll learn that will enable you to take control of the ACT.

You'll Learn the Test Format

The ACT is very predictable. You'd think the test makers would get bored after a while, but they don't. The same kinds of questions, testing the same skills and concepts, appear every time the ACT is given.

Because the test specifications rarely change, you should know in advance what to expect on every section. Just a little familiarity with the directions and common question types can make an enormous difference.

You'll Learn Test Strategies

The ACT isn't a normal exam. Normal exams test mostly your memory. But the ACT tests problem-solving skills as well as memory, and it does so in a standardized test format. That makes the test highly vulnerable to test-smart strategies and techniques.

Most students miss a lot of ACT questions for no good reason. They see a tough looking question, say to themselves, "Uh-oh, I don't remember how to do that," and start to gnaw on their No. 2 pencils.

But many ACT questions can be answered without perfect knowledge of the material being tested. Often, all you need to do to succeed is to think strategically and creatively.

You'll Learn the Concepts Tested

The ACT is designed to test skills and concepts learned in high school and needed for college. Familiarity with the test, coupled with smart test-taking strategies, will take you only so far. For your best score you need to sharpen the skills and knowledge that the ACT rewards. In other words, sometimes you've just got to eat your spinach.

KAPLAN

The good news is that most ACT content is pretty basic. You've probably already learned most of what the ACT expects you to know. But you may need help remembering. That's partly what this book is for—to remind you of the knowledge you already have and to build and refine the specific skills you've developed in high school.

In sum, then, follow these three principles:

- Learn the test format
- Learn test strategies
- Learn the concepts tested

and you'll find yourself just where you should be on test day—in full command of your ACT test taking experience.

> **TO TAKE FULL CONTROL OF THE ACT, YOU'VE GOT TO LEARN THE TEST FORMAT, TEST STRATEGIES, AND CONCEPTS TESTED.**

WHAT IS THE ACT?

Okay, let's start with the basics. The ACT is a three-hour exam (two hours and 55 minutes, to be precise) taken by high school juniors and seniors for admission to college. Contrary to the myths you may have heard, the ACT is not an IQ test. It's a test of problem-solving skills—which means that you can improve your performance by preparing for it.

The ACT consists of four subject tests: English, Math, Reading, and Science Reasoning. All four subject tests are designed primarily to test skills rather than knowledge, though some knowledge is required—particularly in English, for which grammar and writing mechanics is important, and in Math, for which you need to know the basic math concepts taught in a regular high school curriculum.

The ACT:

- Is about three hours long.
- Includes a short break (between the second and third subtests).
- Consists of a total of 215 scored questions.
- Comprises four subject tests:

English	(45 minutes, 75 questions)
Math	(60 minutes, 60 questions)
Reading	(35 minutes, 40 questions)
Science Reasoning	(35 minutes, 40 questions)

HOW IS THE ACT SCORED?

No, your ACT score is not merely the sum total of questions you get right. That would be too simple. Instead, what the test makers do is add up all of your correct answers to get what they call a "raw score." Then they put that raw score into a very large computer, which proceeds to shake, rattle, smoke, and wheeze before spitting out an official score at the other end. That score—which has been put through what they call a scoring formula—is your "scaled score."

ACT scaled scores range from 1 to 36. Nearly half of all test takers score within a much narrower range: 17 to 23. Tests at different dates vary slightly, but the following data are typical.

KAPLAN

Percentile Rank*	Scaled (or Composite) Score	Approximate Percentage Correct
99%	31	90%
90%	26	75%
76%	23	63%
54%	20	53%
28%	17	43%

*Percentage of ACT takers scoring at or below given score

Notice that to earn a score of 20 (the national average), you need to answer only about 53 percent of the questions correct. On most tests, getting only a bit more than half the questions right would be terrible. Not so on the ACT. That fact alone should ease some of your anxiety about how hard this test is. You can miss loads of ACT questions and still get a good score. Nobody expects you to get all of the questions right.

YOU CAN GET A LOT OF QUESTIONS WRONG AND STILL GET A GREAT SCORE.

HOW MANY ACT SCORES WILL YOU GET?

The "ACT scaled score" we've talked about so far is technically called the "composite score." It's the really important one. But when you take the ACT, you actually receive 12 (count 'em, 12) different scores: the composite score, four subject scores, and seven sub-scores.

Below is a breakdown of the subject scores and subscores. Though the four subject scores can play a role in decisions at some schools, the seven subscores usually aren't important for most people:

1. English Score (1–36)
   - Usage/Mechanics Subscore (1–18)
   - Rhetorical Skills Subscore (1–18)

2. Math Score (1–36)
   - Prealgebra/Elementary Algebra Subscore (1–18)
   - Algebra/Coordinate Geometry Subscore (1–18)
   - Plane Geometry/Trigonometry Subscore (1–18)

3. Reading Score (1–36)
   - Social Sciences/Sciences Subscore (1–18)
   - Arts/Literature Subscore (1–18)

4. Science Reasoning Score (1–36)
   (There are no subscores in Science Reasoning.)

HOW DO COLLEGES USE YOUR ACT SCORE?

You may have heard that the ACT is really the only thing colleges look at when deciding whether to admit you. Untrue. Most admissions officers say the ACT is only one of several factors they take into consideration. But let's be realistic. Here's this neat and easy way of comparing all students numerically, no matter what their academic backgrounds and no matter how much grade inflation exists at their high schools. You know the admissions people are going to take a serious look at your scores.

The most important score, naturally, is the composite score (which is an average of the four subject scores). This is the score used by most colleges and universities in the admissions process, and the one that you'll want to mention casually at parties during your freshman year of college. The four subject scores and seven subscores may be used for advanced placement or occasionally for scholarships, but are primarily used by college advisors to help students select majors and first-year courses.

Although many schools deny that they use benchmark scores as cutoffs, we're not sure we really believe them. Big Ten universities and colleges with similarly competitive admissions generally decline to accept students with Composite Scores below 22 or 23. For less competitive schools, the benchmark score may be lower than that; for some very strong schools, the cutoff may be higher.

To be fair, no school uses the ACT score as an absolute bar to admission, no matter how low it is. But for most applicants, a low ACT score is decisive. As a rule, only students whose backgrounds are extremely unusual or who have overcome enormous disadvantages are accepted if their ACT scores are below the benchmark.

SHOULD YOU GUESS ON THE ACT?

The short answer? Yes! The long answer? Yes, of course!

As we said, ACT scores are based on the number of correct answers only. This means that questions left blank and questions answered incorrectly simply don't count. Unlike some other standardized tests, the ACT has no wrong-answer penalty. That's why you should always guess on every ACT question you can't answer, even if you don't have time to read it. Though the questions vary enormously in difficulty, harder questions are worth exactly the same as easier ones, so it pays to guess on the really hard questions and spend your time breezing through the really easy ones. We'll show you just how to do this in the step called "The Top 10 Strategies."

NEVER LEAVE A QUESTION BLANK. IF YOU CAN'T ANSWER A QUESTION—OR DON'T HAVE TIME TO GET TO IT—GUESS.

CAN YOU RETAKE THE TEST?

You can take the ACT as many times as you like. You can then select whichever test score you prefer to be sent to colleges when you apply.

When you sign up for the ACT, you have the option of designating colleges to receive your score. Think twice before you do it! Wait until you receive your score, then send it along if you're happy. This may cost you a few extra dollars (since you won't get to take advantage of the three free reports you get if you designate schools on the registration form before the test), but we think it's worth the extra expense. If you hate your score, you can take the test again and send only the new, improved score. (Seniors, beware! Make sure there is enough time to get your scores in by the application deadline.)

DON'T AUTOMATICALLY DESIGNATE COLLEGES TO RECEIVE SCORE REPORTS AT THE TIME OF REGISTRATION. IF YOU HAVE TIME, WAIT UNTIL YOU'RE SURE YOU'VE GOTTEN A SCORE YOU'RE PROUD OF.

What this means, of course, is that even if you blow the ACT once, you can give yourself another shot without the schools of your choice knowing about it. The ACT is one of the few areas of your academic life in which you get a second chance.

KAPLAN

STEP 2:
THE FOUR SUBJECT TESTS

Okay, you've seen how the ACT is set up. But to really know the test, you've got to know something about the four ACT subject tests (which, by the way, always appear in the following order):

- English
- Mathematics
- Reading
- Science Reasoning

As we'll see, the questions in every subject test vary widely in difficulty. Some are so easy that most elementary school students could answer them. Others might give even college students a little trouble. But, again, the questions are not arranged in order of difficulty. That's different from some other tests, in which easier questions come first. Skipping past hard questions is important, since otherwise you may never reach easy ones at the end of the exam.

> **SKIP PAST HARD QUESTIONS SO THAT YOU CAN QUICKLY RACK UP POINTS ON EASIER QUESTIONS.**

Here's a preview of the types of questions you'll encounter on the four subject tests. We'll keep the questions toward the easy end of the difficulty scale here, since you're just becoming familiar with the test. Later, we'll be less kind.

THE ENGLISH SUBJECT TEST

STATISTIC: The English test is 45 minutes long and includes 75 questions. That works out to about 30 seconds per question. The test is divided into five passages, each with about 15 questions.

Students nearly always get more questions correct in English than in any other section. That tends to make students think that English is a lot easier than the rest of the ACT. But, alas, it's not that simple. Because most students do well, the test makers have much higher expectations for English than for other parts of the test. That's why, to earn an average English subscore (a 20, say), you have to get almost two-thirds of the questions right, while on the rest of the test you need to get only about half right.

Note too that you have less time per question on the English test than on any of the other three tests. You'll have to move fast.

NEVER SPEND MORE THAN 45 SECONDS OR SO ON AN ENGLISH QUESTION.

The Format

Almost all of the English questions follow a standard format. A word, phrase, or sentence in a passage is underlined. You're given four options: to leave the underlined portion alone ("NO CHANGE," which is always the first choice), or to replace it with one of three alternatives. For example:

. . . Pike's Peak in Southwest

Colorado is named <u>before Zebulon</u>
              37
<u>Pike, an early explorer.</u> He traveled
     37
through the area, exploring ...

37. A NO CHANGE
    B. before Zebulon Pike
       became an explorer,
    C. after Zebulon Pike,
       when,
    D. after Zebulon Pike.

KAPLAN

The best answer choice is D. The other choices all have various problems—grammatical, stylistic, logical. They make the passage look and sound as if it were written by your baby brother.

IN ENGLISH, TRUST YOUR EARS. THE RIGHT ANSWER IS USUALLY THE ONE THAT "SOUNDS RIGHT" TO YOU.

Notice that a single question can test different kinds of writing errors. We find that about one-third of the English questions test writing economy (we call them Economy questions), about another third test for logic and sense (Sense questions), and the remaining third test hard-and-fast rules of grammar (Technicality questions). There's overlap between these question types, so don't worry too much about categories. We provide them to give you an idea of the kinds of errors you'll be expected to correct.

The Directions

The directions on the English test illustrate why there's an advantage to knowing the directions before test day. The English directions are long and complicated. We're going to show you what they look like, but take our advice: Don't bother reading them. We'll show you exactly what you need to do. Then, while everyone else is reading the directions on the day of the test, you'll be racking up points.

Directions: In the following five passages, certain words and phrases have been underlined and numbered. You will find alternatives for each underlined portion in the right-hand column. Select the one that best expresses the idea, that makes the statement acceptable in standard written English, or that is phrased most consistently with the style and tone of the entire passage. If you feel that the original version is best, select "NO CHANGE." You will also find questions asking about a section of the passage or about the entire passage.

For these questions decide which choice gives the most appropriate response to the given question. For each question in the test, select the best choice and fill in the corresponding space on the answer folder. You may wish to read each passage through before you begin to answer the questions associated with it. Most answers cannot be determined without reading several sentences around the phrases in question. Make sure to read far enough ahead each time you choose an alternative.

You read the directions anyway, didn't you? Well, that's okay. You'll never have to do it again.

DON'T WASTE TIME READING DIRECTIONS ON TEST DAY.

To Omit or Not to Omit

Some English questions offer, as one alternative, the chance to completely omit the underlined portion, usually as the last of the four choices. For example:

. . . Later, Pike fell while valiantly

defending America in the War

of 1812. <u>It goes without saying</u>
            40
<u>that this took place after he</u>
            40
<u>discovered Pike's Peak.</u> He
            40
actually died near York (now

called Toronto). . . .

40. F. NO CHANGE
    G. Clearly, this must have occurred subsequent to his discovering Pike's Peak.
    H. This was after he found Pike's Peak.
    J. OMIT the underlined portion.

In this case, J is correct. The idea really does "go without saying," so it shouldn't be stated. On recent ACTs, when OMIT has appeared as an answer choice, it's been correct more than half the time. Don't always select OMIT, however, since it's also been wrong almost half of the time.

KAPLAN

Nonstandard Format Questions

Some English questions—usually about 10 per exam—don't follow this standard format. These items pose a question and offer four possible responses. In many cases, the responses are either "yes" or "no," with an explanation. Pay attention to the reasoning.

. . . Later, Pike fell while valiantly

defending America in the War

of 1812. [40] He actually died

near York (now called Toronto). . . .

40. Suppose the author considered adding the following sentence at this point:

"It goes without saying that this occurred after he discovered Pike's Peak." Given the overall purpose of the passage, would this sentence be appropriate?

F. No, because the sentence adds nothing to the meaning of the passage.

G. No, because the passage is not concerned with Pike's achievements.

H. Yes, because otherwise the sequence of events would be unclear.

J. Yes; though the sentence is not needed, the author recognizes this fact by using the phrase "it goes without saying."

The correct answer for question 40 is F. Though G correctly indicates that the sentence doesn't belong in the passage, it offers a pretty inappropriate reason. Choices H and J, meanwhile, are wrong because they recommend including a sentence that's clearly redundant.

Many of the nonstandard questions occur at the end of a passage. Some ask about the meaning, purpose, or tone of the text. Others ask you to evaluate it, and still others ask you to determine the proper order of words, sentences, or paragraphs that have been scrambled.

We think you'll like the English subject test. It can actually be fun, which is probably why the test makers put it first. We'll cover strategies for the question types in the two English steps later.

THE MATHEMATICS SUBJECT TEST

STATISTIC: The Math test is 60 minutes long and includes 60 questions. That works out to a minute a question, but some will take more time than that, some less.

The Format

All of the math questions have the same multiple-choice format. They ask a question and offer five possible choices (unlike questions on the other three subject tests, which have only *four* choices each).

MATH IS THE ONLY SUBJECT TEST THAT HAS FIVE ANSWER CHOICES, RATHER THAN FOUR.

The questions cover a full range of math topics, from prealgebra and elementary algebra through intermediate algebra, coordinate geometry, plane geometry, and even trigonometry.

Although the math questions, like those in other sections, aren't ordered in terms of difficulty, questions drawn from the elementary school or junior high curricula tend to come earlier in the section, while those from high school curricula tend to come later. But this doesn't mean that the easy questions come first and the hardest ones come later. We've found that high school subjects tend to be fresher in most students' minds than things they were taught years ago, so you may actually find the later questions easier.

> **DON'T ASSUME THAT ALL OF THE EASY QUESTIONS COME EARLY IN A SUBJECT TEST.**

The Directions

Here's what the math directions will look like:

> **Directions:** Solve each of the following problems, select the correct answer, and then fill in the corresponding space on your answer sheet.
>
> Don't linger over problems that are too time-consuming. Do as many as you can, then come back to the others in the time you have remaining.
>
> Note: Unless otherwise noted, all of the following should be assumed.
>
> 1. Illustrative figures are not necessarily drawn to scale.
>
> 2. All geometric figures lie in a plane.
>
> 3. The term *line* indicates a straight line.
>
> 4. The term *average* indicates arithmetic mean.

Again, when it comes to directions on the ACT, the golden rule is: Don't read them! You'll already know what they say by the time you take the test.

The math directions don't really tell you much anyway. Of the four special notes at the end of the math directions, numbers 2, 3, and 4 almost go without saying. Note 1—that figures are not necessarily drawn to scale—seems pretty scary, but in fact the vast majority of

ACT figures are drawn to scale (a fact that, as we'll see, has signifi-cant implications for how to guess on geometry questions).

Reading and Drawing Diagrams

We find that about one-third of the math questions either give you a diagram or describe a situation that should be diagrammed. For these questions, the diagrams are crucial. For example:

1. The figure below contains five congruent triangles. The longest side of each triangle is 4 meters long. What is the area of the whole figure?

A. 12.5 square meters

B. 15 square meters

C. 20 square meters

D. 30 square meters

E. Cannot be determined from the given information

The key to this question is to let the diagram tell you what you need to know—that each triangle represents one-quarter of the area of the square, and that the sides of the square are 4 meters (you can figure this out because the top side of the square is the hypotenuse—or longest side—of the triangle that makes the "roof"). Since the area of a square can be found by squaring the side, the area of the square is 16 square meters. Thus, each triangle has an area one-fourth as much—4 square meters. Since the whole figure consists of five triangles, each with area 4, the total area is $5 \times 4 = 20$. The answer is C.

How to Get That Story

We find that about another third of the math questions are story problems like the following:

2. Evan drove halfway home at 20 miles per hour, then sped up and drove the rest of the way at 30 miles per hour. What was his average speed for the entire trip?

    F. 20 miles per hour

    G. 22 miles per hour

    H. 24 miles per hour

    J. 25 miles per hour

    K. 28 miles per hour

A good way to comprehend—and resolve—a story problem like this is to think of a real situation that's similar. For example, what if Evan had 120 miles to drive? (It helps to pick a distance that's easily divisible by both rates.) He would go 60 miles at 30 mph, then 60 miles at 20 mph. How long would it take? 60 miles at 30 mph is 2 hours; 60 miles at 20 mph is 3 hours. That's a total of 120 miles in 5 hours; 120 divided by 5 gives an average speed of 24 mph. The correct answer is thus H. (Note: We'll show you alternative ways to answer questions like this later.)

Getting the Concept

Finally, we find that about one-third of the math questions directly ask you to demonstrate your knowledge of specific math concepts. For example:

3. If angles *A* and *B* are supplementary, and the measure of angle *A* is 57°, what is the measure, in degrees, of angle *B* ?

   A. 33
   B. 43
   C. 47
   D. 123
   E. 147

This question simply requires that you know the concept of "supplementary angles." Two angles are supplementary when they form a straight line—in other words, when they add up to 180°. Thus, Question 3 boils down to this: What number, added to 57, makes 180? The answer is D.

These three types of math questions, of course, will be discussed more fully in the three math steps.

THE READING SUBJECT TEST

STATISTIC: The Reading test is 35 minutes long and includes 40 questions. The test contains four passages, each of which is followed by 10 questions. When you factor out the amount of time you'll initially spend on the passages, this works out to about 30 seconds per question—again, more for some, less for others.

The Format

There are four categories of reading passages: Social Studies, Natural Sciences, Humanities, and Prose Fiction. You'll get one passage in each category. The passages are about 1,000 words long and are written at about the same difficulty level as college textbooks and readings.

The Social Studies, Natural Sciences, and Humanities passages are usually well-organized essays. Each has a very specific theme. Questions expect you to recognize this theme, to comprehend specific facts contained in the passage, and to understand the structure of the essay. Prose Fiction passages require you to understand the thoughts, feelings, and motivations of fictional characters, even when these are not explicitly stated in the passage.

Whatever the type of passage, it's important that you skim it quickly rather than read it carefully. It's crucial that you not get bogged down. Remember that you can always deal with the details later, if and when they become relevant in the questions.

SKIM ALL READING PASSAGES; DO NOT READ THEM CAREFULLY!

After each passage, you'll find 10 questions. There are really only three different categories of Reading questions:

- Specific Detail questions
- Inference questions
- Big Picture questions

The Directions

Here's what the reading directions will look like:

Directions: This test contains four passages, each followed by several questions. After reading a passage, select the best answer to each question and fill in the corresponding oval on your answer sheet. You are allowed to refer to the passages while answering the questions.

Nothing stupefying here. But nothing very substantive, either. We'll be a little more specific and strategic than the test makers are when we suggest a plan of attack in the two reading steps.

Reading Passages

What follows is a sample reading minipassage. Note that this passage is much shorter than the ones you'll see on the test. We provide it here to give you an idea of the kind of material you'll be encountering, and to generate material for the three sample reading questions that follow. In the two reading steps later on, we'll give you a full-length reading passage, with questions.

> Recent geological studies have demonstrated the existence of huge deposits of gas hydrate, a frozen compound consisting of flammable methane gas trapped in ice, on continental shelves around the globe. These deposits, which exist under extreme pressure at a depth of 1,500 feet under the ocean floor, are believed to contain twice as much potential carbon energy as all fossil fuels combined. Efforts to mine this "burnable ice," however, will pose one of the great engineering problems of the next century. Ocean floor avalanches, set off by mining activity, could conceivably release vast amounts of methane into the atmosphere, setting off an intensified "greenhouse effect" that could significantly alter the world's climate.

Nailing Down the Details

Here's a Specific Detail question that might come after the minipassage above:

1. According to the passage, a major obstacle to the successful mining of gas hydrate is:

   A. the inaccessibility of the deposits.

   B. recent climatic changes caused by the "greenhouse effect."

   C. the potential of mining accidents to cause environmental harm.

   D. the danger posed by methane gas to the health of minors.

Specific Detail questions ask about things stated explicitly in the passage. The challenge with them is, first, finding the proper place in the passage where the answer can be found (sometimes you'll be given a line reference, sometimes not), and second, being able to match up what you see in the passage with the correct answer, which will probably be worded differently.

In this question, the mention of the "major obstacle" in the question stem should have led you to the last sentence in the passage, where the potential problems of gas hydrate mining are specified. And the problem mentioned there is avalanches (mining accidents) and the subsequent release of methane into the atmosphere (environmental harm). That's why C is correct here.

Notice how some wrong choices are designed to trip you up by including details from other parts of the passage, or by using the same wording that the passage uses while distorting the meaning.

Making an Inference

We find that most reading passages also include a large number of Inference questions, which require you to make an inference from the passage (to "read between the lines"). They differ somewhat from Specific Detail questions. For one thing, students usually consider them harder.

Here's a sample Inference question relating to our minipassage:

2. It can be inferred that gas hydrate can be used for energy because it:

    F. is under great pressure.

    G. contains gas that can be burned.

    H. will contribute to the greenhouse effect.

    J. is frozen.

 23

Here you have to put two and two together to get your answer. You're told that gas hydrate contains "flammable methane gas." Later, the gas hydrate is referred to as "burnable ice." Since ice is not normally burnable, it must be the methane in the ice that allows it to be burned, creating energy. G is correct.

Getting the Big Picture

Although the majority of reading questions are Specific Detail and Inference questions like those above, some will be what we call Big Picture questions. Some Big Picture questions ask about the passage as a whole, requiring you to find the theme, tone, or structure of the passage. Others ask you to evaluate the writing.

Here's a sample Big Picture question:

3. The author's main purpose in the passage above is to do which of the following?

A. advocate the mining of gas hydrate deposits

B. show how scientists are looking for alternatives to fossil fuels

C. argue that the risks of deep-sea mining are too great

D. describe a potential new energy source

The best choice here is D, since it is general enough to describe the full passage (the potential new energy source being gas hydrate), but it's not overly general or broad (like B), and it doesn't introduce value judgments that are not really present in the passage (as A and C do, by implying that the author either advocates or condemns gas hydrate mining).

We'll discuss strategies for all passage types and question types in the two reading steps.

THE SCIENCE REASONING SUBJECT TEST

STATISTIC: The Science Reasoning test is 35 minutes long and includes 40 questions. The test contains seven passages, each followed by five to seven questions. Factoring out the amount of time you'll initially spend on the passage leaves you a little more than 30 seconds for each question.

No, you don't have to be a scientist to succeed on the ACT Science Reasoning test. All that's required is common sense (though a knowledge of standard scientific processes and procedures sure does help). You'll be given passages containing various kinds of scientific information—drawn from the fields of biology, chemistry, physics, geology, astronomy, and meteorology—that you'll have to understand and use as a basis for inferences.

The Format

On most science reasoning tests, three passages present scientific data and three passages discuss specific experiments. In addition, there's usually one passage in which two scientists state opposing views on the same issue. Each passage will generate five to seven questions. A warning: Some of these passages will be very difficult to understand, but to make up for that fact, there will be easy questions attached to them. The test makers do show a little mercy once in a while.

SEEK OUT EASY QUESTIONS. THEY EXIST ON EVEN THE HARDEST SCIENCE REASONING PASSAGES.

The Directions

Here's what the Science Reasoning directions will look like:

Directions: Each of the following seven passages is followed by several questions. After reading each passage, decide on the best answer to each question and fill in the corresponding oval on your answer sheet. You are allowed to refer to the passages while answering the questions.

Sounds a lot like the set of directions for Reading, doesn't it? Not much substance here, either. But don't worry. We'll show you the best strategic way to attack the science reasoning subject test in the three Science steps.

Analyzing Data

About one-third of the questions on the Science Reasoning test require you to read data from graphs or tables. In easier questions, you'll need only to report the information. In harder questions, you may need to draw inferences or note patterns in the data. For example:

TYPICAL PERFORMANCE ON SCIENCE REASONING QUESTIONS

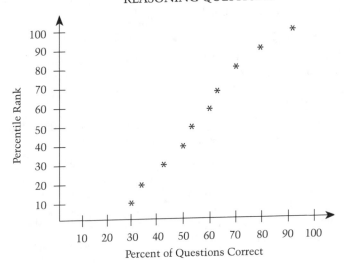

1. A test taker who scores in approximately the 40th percentile has correctly answered about what fraction of the questions?

    A. $\frac{9}{10}$

    B. $\frac{2}{3}$

    C. $\frac{1}{2}$

    D. $\frac{1}{5}$

The correct answer is C. The point with 40th percentile as its y-coordinate has an x-coordinate approximately above the 50 percent point on the horizontal axis (percent correct). 50 percent is the same as $\frac{1}{2}$. Note that this question involves a little simple arithmetic (translating a percent into a fraction)—not uncommon for Science Reasoning questions.

Conducting Experiments

Other Science Reasoning questions require that you understand how experiments are designed and what they prove.

A scientist adds one drop of nitric acid to beakers A, B, and C. Each beaker contains water from a different stream. The water in beaker A came from Stream A, that in beaker B came from Stream B, and that in beaker C came from Stream C. In beakers B and C, small precipitates form, but not in beaker A.

12. Which of the following could properly be inferred on the basis of the experiment?

F. Stream A is more polluted than Streams B or C.

G. Streams B and C are more polluted than Stream A.

H. Stream A contains material that neutralizes nitric acid.

J. Streams B and C contain some substance that reacts in the presence of nitric acid.

The correct answer is J. Since a precipitate forms when nitric acid is added to beakers B and C, which contain water from streams B and C, something in these streams must be involved. However, we don't know that it is pollution, so answers F and G are unwarranted. We also don't know exactly why no precipitate formed in beaker A, so H is also an unwarranted conclusion.

The Principle of the Thing

The remaining Science Reasoning questions require you either to apply a principle logically, or to identify ways to defend or attack a principle. Some questions will involve two scientists stating opposing views on the same subject. Or, a passage might describe a theory about how "V-shaped" valleys are typically formed on Earth—by water erosion through soft rock. Then the following question might be asked:

16. Which of the following is most likely to be a V-shaped valley?

    F. A valley formed by glaciers

    G. A river valley that is cut into very hard basalt

    H. A valley formed by wind erosion

    J. A river valley in a region of soft shale rocks

The correct answer is J, since this is consistent with the passage as described.

STEP 3:
THE TOP TEN STRATEGIES

Now that you have some idea of the kind of adversary you face in the ACT, it's time to start developing strategies for dealing with this adversary. Here are the top ten general test strategies for success on the ACT.

1. DO QUESTION TRIAGE

In a hospital emergency room, the triage nurse is the person who evaluates each patient and decides which ones get attention first and which ones should be treated later. You should do the same thing on the ACT.

Performing question triage is one of the most important ways of controlling your test-taking experience. There are some questions on the ACT that most students could never answer correctly, no matter how much time or effort they spent on them. For example:

57. If $\sec^2 x = 4$, which of the following could be $\sin x$?

      A. 1.73205

      B. 3.14159

      C. $\sqrt{3}$

      D. $\dfrac{\sqrt{3}}{2}$

      E. Cannot be determined from the given information.

Clearly, even if you could manage to come up with an answer to this question, it would take some time. But would it be worth the time? We think not.

This question clearly illustrates our point: You should perform question triage on the ACT. The first time you look at each question, make a quick decision about how hard and time-consuming it looks. Then decide whether to answer it now or skip it and do it later. Here's how:

- If the question looks comprehensible and of reasonable difficulty, do it right away.
- If the question looks tough and time-consuming, but ultimately "doable," skip it, circle the question number and come back to it later.
- If the question looks impossible, forget about it. Guess and move on, never to return.

This triage method will ensure you spend the time needed to do all the basic questions before you get bogged down with the tough problems. Remember, every question is worth the same number of points. You get no extra credit for test machismo.

For the English, Reading, and Science Reasoning sections, the best plan of attack is to do each passage as a block. Make a longish first pass through the questions (the "triage" pass), doing the easy ones, guessing on the impossible ones, and skipping any that look like they might cause trouble. Then, make a second pass (the "cleanup" pass) and do those questions you think you can solve with some elbow grease. This will be easier if you've marked these questions in your test booklet. For Math, you use the same two-pass strategy, except that you move through the whole subject test twice.

MAKE TWO PASSES THROUGH EACH GROUP OF QUESTIONS—
A TRIAGE PASS AND A CLEANUP PASS.

No matter what subject test you're working on, you should take pains to grid your answers in the right place. It's easy to misgrid when you're skipping around, so be careful. And of course: Make sure you have an answer gridded for every question by the time the test is over!

2. PUT THE MATERIAL INTO A FORM YOU CAN UNDERSTAND

ACT questions are rarely presented in the simplest, most helpful way. In fact, your main job for many questions is to figure out what the question means so you can solve it.

Since the material is presented in such an intimidating way, one of your best strategies for taking control is to recast (reword) the material into a form you can handle better.

Mark Up Your Test Booklet

This strategy should be employed on all four subject tests. For example, in Reading many students find the passages overwhelming. There are 85 to 90 lines of dense verbiage for each one! But the secret is to put the passages into a form you can understand and use. Circle or underline the main idea, for one thing. And make yourself a road map of the passage, making brief notes about each paragraph so you understand how it all fits together. That way, you'll also know *where* to find certain types of information you'll need.

Part One: Preparing for the ACT

Reword the Questions

You'll find that you also need to do some recasting of the questions. For instance, take the following question stem from a Science Reasoning passage.

15. According to Figure 1, at approximately what latitude would calculations using an estimated value at sea level of $g = 9.80$ m/sec^2 produce the least error?

    A. 0°

    B. 20°

    C. 40°

    D. 80°

Figure 1

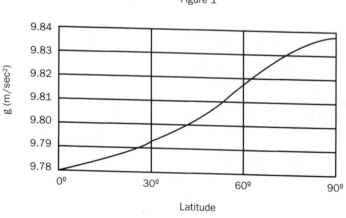

Latitude

At what latitude would the calculations using a value of $g = 9.80$ m/sec^2 produce the least error? Yikes! What does that mean?

Take a deep breath. Ask yourself: Where would an estimate of 9.80 m/sec^2 produce the least error? In a latitude where 9.80 m/sec^2 is the real value of g. If you find the latitude at which the real value of g is 9.80 m/sec^2, then using 9.80 m/sec^2 as an estimate there would produce no error at all!

So, in other words, what this question is asking is: At what latitude does $g = 9.80$ m/sec^2? Now that's a form of the question you can understand. In that form, you can answer it easily. The answer is choice C, which you can get just by reading the chart.

Draw Diagrams

Sometimes, putting the material into usable form involves drawing with your pencil. For instance, take another math problem:

2. Jason bought a painting with a frame 1 inch wide. If the dimensions of the outside of the frame are 5 inches by 7 inches, which of the following could be the length of one of the sides of the painting inside the frame?

   F. 3 inches

   G. 4 inches

   H. $5\frac{1}{2}$ inches

   J. $6\frac{1}{2}$ inches

   K. 7 inches

Just looking at the question the first time, you might be tempted simply to subtract 1 inch from the outside dimensions and think that the inside dimensions are 4 by 6 inches (and pick G). Why isn't this correct? Because the frame goes all the way around—both above and below the painting, both to the right and to the left. This would have been clear if you had put the problem in a form you could understand and use.

For instance, you might have made the situation graphic by actually sketching out the painting frame:

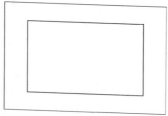

When you draw the picture frame like this, you realize that if the outside dimensions are 5 by 7 inches, the inside dimensions must be 3 by 5 inches. Thus, the correct answer is F.

PUT EVERYTHING INTO A FORM YOU CAN UNDERSTAND.

3. IGNORE IRRELEVANT ISSUES

It's easy to waste time on ACT questions by considering irrelevant issues. Just because an issue looks interesting, or just because you're worried about something, doesn't make it important. For example:

. . . China was certainly one of

the cradles of civilization. <u>It's</u>
                 14

<u>obvious that, China has a long</u>
        14

<u>history.</u> As is the case with
   14

other ancient cultures, the early

history of China is lost in

mythology. . . .

14. F. NO CHANGE
    G. It's obvious that China has a long history.
    H. Obviously, China has a long history.
    J. OMIT the underlined portion.

In this question, the test makers are counting on you to waste time worrying about punctuation. Does that comma belong? Can you use a semicolon here? These issues might be worrisome, but there's a much bigger issue here—namely, does the sentence belong in the passage at all? No, it doesn't. If China has an ancient culture and was a cradle of civilization, it must have a long history, so the sentence really is "obvious." Redundancy is the relevant issue here, not punctuation. Choice J is correct.

DON'T GET CAUGHT UP IN ISSUES THAT WON'T GET YOU A POINT.

4. CHECK BACK

Remember, all of the information you need is in the test itself. You shouldn't be afraid to refer to it.

In Reading and Science Reasoning, always refer to the place in the passage where the answer to a question can be found (the question stem will often contain a line reference or a reference to a specific table, graph, or experiment to help you out). Your chosen answer should match the passage—not in exact vocabulary or units of measurement, perhaps, but in meaning.

Checking back is especially important in Reading and Science Reasoning, because the passages leave many people feeling adrift in a sea of details. Often, the wrong answers will be "misplaced details"—details taken from different parts of the passage. These misplaced details don't answer the question properly but might sound good to you if you aren't careful. By checking back with the passage, you can avoid making such wrong choices.

There's another important lesson here: Don't pick an answer just because it contains "keywords" you remember from the passage. Many wrong answer choices are distortions; they use the right words but say the wrong things about them. Look for choices that contain the same ideas you find in the passage.

> TO AVOID CHOOSING MISPLACED DETAILS AND DISTORTIONS, CHECK BACK WITH THE PASSAGE.

5. ANSWER THE RIGHT QUESTION

This strategy is a natural extension of the last. As we said, the ACT test makers often include among the wrong answers to a question the *correct answer to a different question*. Under time pressure, it's easy for you to fall for one of these red herrings, thinking that you know what's being asked for when you really don't. For example:

7. What is the value of $3x$ if $9x = 5y + 2$ and
    $y + 4 = 2y - 10$?

    A. 5
    B. 8
    C. 14
    D. 24
    E. 72

To solve this problem, we need to find y first, even though the question asks about x (because x here is given only in terms of y). You could solve the second equation like this:

$$y + 4 = 2y - 10 \quad \text{given}$$
$$4 = y - 10 \quad \text{by subtracting } y \text{ from both sides}$$
$$14 = y \quad \text{by adding 10 to both sides}$$

But C, 14, isn't the right answer here, because the question doesn't ask for y—it asks about x. We can use the value of y to find x, however, by plugging the calculated value of y into the first equation:

$$9x = 5y + 2 \quad \text{given}$$
$$9x = 5(14) + 2 \quad \text{because } y = 14$$
$$9x = 70 + 2 \quad 5 \times 14 = 70$$
$$9x = 72$$

But E, 72, isn't the answer either, because the question doesn't ask for $9x$. It doesn't ask for x either, so if you picked B, 8, you'd be wrong as well. Remember to refer to the question! The question asks for $3x$. So we need to divide $9x$ by 3:

$$9x = 72 \qquad \text{from above}$$
$$3x = 24 \qquad \text{dividing by 3}$$

Thus, the answer is D.

Doing all the right work but then getting the wrong answer can be seriously depressing. So be sure to answer the right question.

ALWAYS CHECK THE QUESTION STEM AGAIN BEFORE CHOOSING YOUR ANSWER.

6. LOOK FOR THE HIDDEN ANSWER

On many ACT questions, the right answer is hidden in one way or another. It might be hidden by being written in a way that you aren't likely to expect. For example, you might work out a problem and get .5 as your answer, but then find that .5 isn't among the answer choices. Then you notice that one choice reads " $\frac{1}{2}$."

But there's another way the ACT can hide answers. Many ACT questions have more than one possible right solution, though only one correct answer choice is given. Often, the ACT will hide that answer by offering one of the less obvious possible answers to a question. For example:

2. If $3x^2 + 5 = 17$, which of the following could be the value of x ?

   A. –3

   B. –2

   C. 0

   D. 1

   E. 4

You quickly solve this very straightforward problem like so:

$3x^2 + 5 = 17$	given
$3x^2 = 12$	by subtracting 5
$x^2 = 4$	dividing by 3
$x = 2$	taking square root of both sides

Having arrived at an answer, you confidently look for it among the choices. But 2 isn't a choice. The explanation? This question has two possible solutions, not just one. The square root of 4 can be either 2 or –2, so B is the answer.

Keep in mind that though there is only one right answer choice for each question, that right answer may not be the one that occurs to you first. A common mistake is to pick an answer that seems "sort of" like the answer you're looking for even when you know it's wrong. Don't settle for second best.

> IF YOU DON'T FIND YOUR ANSWER AMONG THE CHOICES,
> TRY TO THINK OF ANOTHER WAY TO ANSWER THE QUESTION.

7. GUESS INTELLIGENTLY

On the ACT, an unanswered question is always wrong, but even a wild guess may be right. In fact, smart guessing can make a big difference in your score. Always guess on every ACT question you can't answer.

You'll be doing two different kinds of guessing during your two sweeps through any subject test:

- Blind guessing (which you do mostly on questions you deem too hard or time-consuming to try)
- Considered guessing (which you do mostly on questions that you do some work on, but can't make headway with)

When you guess blindly, you just choose any letter you feel like choosing. When you guess in a considered way, on the other hand, you've usually done enough work on a question to eliminate at least one or two choices. If you can eliminate any choices, you increase the odds that you'll guess correctly.

> **GUESS IF YOU CAN'T FIGURE OUT AN ANSWER TO A QUESTION!**

8. BE CAREFUL WITH THE ANSWER GRID

Your ACT score is based on the answers you select on your answer grid. Even if you work out every ACT question correctly, you'll get a low score if you misgrid your answers. So be careful! Don't disdain the process of filling in those little "bubbles" on the grid. Sure, it's pretty mindless, but under time pressure it's easy to lose control and make mistakes.

It's important to develop a disciplined strategy for filling in the answer grid. We find that gridding the answers in groups rather than one question at a time works best. As you figure out each question in the test booklet, circle the answer choice you come up with. Then transfer those answers to the answer grid in groups of five or more (until you get close to the end of time for the section, when you start gridding answers one-by-one).

In English, Reading, and Science Reasoning, the test is divided naturally into groups of questions—the passages. For most students, it makes sense to circle your answers in your test booklet as you work them out. Then, when you're finished with each passage and its questions, fill in the answers as a group on your answer grid.

In Math, the strategy has to be different because the Math test isn't broken up into natural groups. The best strategy is to mark your answers in the test booklet and then grid them when you reach the end of each page or two. Since there are usually about five math questions per page, you'll probably be gridding five or ten math answers at a time.

GRID YOUR ANSWERS IN GROUPS.

No matter what subject you're working on, however, you should start gridding your answers one at a time near the end of the session. You don't want to be caught with ungridded answers when time is called.

During each subject test, the proctor should warn you when you have about five minutes left. But don't depend on that! Rely on your own watch: When there are five minutes left in a subject test, start gridding your answers one-by-one. With a minute or two left, fill in everything you've left blank. Remember: Even one question left blank could cut your score.

BE YOUR OWN TIMEKEEPER.

9. USE THE LETTERS OF THE ANSWER CHOICES TO STAY ON TRACK

One oddity about the ACT is that even-numbered questions have F, G, H, J (and, in Math, K) as answer choices, rather than A, B, C, D (and E in Math). This might be confusing at first, but you can make it work for you. A common mistake with the answer grid is to enter an answer one row up or down accidentally. On the ACT, that won't happen if you pay attention to the letter in the answer. If you're looking for an A and you see only F, G, H, J, and K, you'll know you're in the wrong row on the answer grid.

> **KEEP CHECKING THE LETTERS OF YOUR ANSWERS TO AVOID MISGRIDDING.**

10. KEEP TRACK OF TIME

It's important to keep track of time while you take the ACT. During your two passes through each subject test, you really have to pace yourself. On average, English, Reading, and Science Reasoning questions should take about one-half minute each. Math questions should average less than one minute each.

Set your watch to 12:00 at the beginning of each subject test, so it will be easy to check your time. Again, don't rely on proctors, even if they promise that they'll dutifully call out the time every five, ten, or fifteen minutes. Proctors get distracted once in a while.

For English, Reading, and Science Reasoning questions, it's useful to check your timing as you grid the answers for each passage. English and Reading passages should take about nine minutes each. Science Reasoning passages should average about five minutes.

Remember that more basic questions should take less time, and harder ones will probably take more. In Math, for instance, you need to go much faster than one per minute during your first sweep. But at the end, you may spend two or three minutes on each of the hardest problems you work out.

> **CHECK YOUR TIME AT FREQUENT, NATURAL INTERVALS.**

TAKE CONTROL

A common thread in all 10 strategies above is: Take control. You are the master of the test-taking experience. Do the questions in the order you want and in the way you want. Use your time for one purpose—to maximize your score. Don't get bogged down or agonize. Remember, you don't earn points for suffering, but you do earn points for moving on to the next question and getting it right.

In the remaining steps of your study program, we'll provide you with the arsenal of tools and techniques you'll need to take control of all four subject tests on the ACT.

THE ACT
ENGLISH TEST

STEP 4:
BASIC ENGLISH SKILLS

Almost all of us have padded papers at one time or another in our academic careers. The recipe for padding, in fact, is practically universal: You repeat yourself a few times. You trade short phrases for long-winded verbiage. You add a few offbeat ideas that don't really belong. And presto! Your six-page paper is transformed into a 10-page paper.

The ACT test makers know that most students pad when they write. And on the English subject test, they know how to punish you for it. In fact, almost one-third of the English questions on the ACT—we call them Economy questions—are testing for long-windedness, repetition, and irrelevance.

But there's hope. Once you know what ACT English is testing for, you can easily avoid making these common English mistakes. More than any other part of the exam, ACT English is predictable.

SKIMMING ENGLISH PASSAGES

Before launching in and starting to correct the prose on an ACT English passage, it usually pays to skim each paragraph to get a sense of how it's shaped and what it's about. For most students, that makes correcting the underlined portions a little easier, since you'll have a better sense of the context. The skimming technique is simple: You skim a paragraph, then do the questions it contains, then skim the next paragraph, do the questions it contains, and so forth. Some students even find it helpful to skim the entire passage before starting on the questions.

In this preliminary skim, you needn't read carefully—you'll be doing that when you tackle the questions—but you should get a sense of what the passage is about and, just as important, whether it's written in a formal or informal style.

After your brief skim of a paragraph (it should take only a few seconds), it's time to start work on its questions.

> TRY SKIMMING AN ENGLISH PASSAGE BEFORE STARTING
> WORK ON THE QUESTIONS.

ECONOMY QUESTIONS

Try your hand at the following English minipassage—and pay attention to the message conveyed as well.

On recent ACTs, the shortest answer is

correct and absolutely right, for about
          1
half of all English questions. Because this

1. A. NO CHANGE
   B. correct
   C. right, that is, correct,
   D. correct, absolutely, and

   (A) (B) (C) (D)

is <u>true</u>, a student who knew no English
     2

2. F. NO CHANGE
   G. truthfully factual
   H. factually correct
   J. factual—and true too—

   (F) (G) (H) (J)

at all could earn—and justly so—an
3
English subject score of about 15. Such

a student could compare the choices

carefully, and choose the single
4
shortest one every time. Where the
4
answers were same length, the

the student could pick at random. On

recent published ACTs, guessing in this

way would have yielded between 35 and

38 correct answers out of 75 questions

(The SAT doesn't have an English section,
5
so this advice won't work on that test).
5

3. A NO CHANGE
   B. , and justly so,
   C. and justify
   D. OMIT the
       underlined portion.
       Ⓐ Ⓑ Ⓒ Ⓓ

4. F. NO CHANGE
   G. singularly shortest
       one
   H. uniquely short
       item
   J. shortest one
       Ⓕ Ⓖ Ⓗ Ⓙ

5. A. NO CHANGE
   B. The SAT doesn't
       have an English
       section.
   C. This doesn't work
       on the SAT.
   D. OMIT the
       underlined portion
       and end the
       sentence with a
       period.
       Ⓐ Ⓑ Ⓒ Ⓓ

Of course, you're going to do much

better than that. You actually <u>are capable</u>

<u>speaking the English Language</u>. You may
6

not know every little rule of English

usage, but you certainly know *something*.

Obviously, getting the question right

6. F. NO CHANGE
   G. of possess the capability of speaking that wonderful language called the language of England
   H. possess the capability of speaking in the land called England
   J. speak English

   Ⓕ Ⓖ Ⓗ Ⓙ

because you *know* the <u>right answer</u>
7
is better than getting it right because

you guessed well. But you should always

remember that the ACT test makers

7. A. NO CHANGE
   B. best choice to select
   C. most correct answer of the choices given
   D. answer considered as correct

   Ⓐ Ⓑ Ⓒ Ⓓ

<u>like</u> the shortest answers.
8

8. F. NO CHANGE
   G. have a habit of liking
   H. habitually tend to like
   J. are in the habit of liking

   Ⓕ Ⓖ Ⓗ Ⓙ

ANSWERS: 1. B, 2. F, 3. D, 4. J, 5. D, 6. J, 7. A, 8. F

In case you didn't notice, the shortest answer happens to be correct in all eight of the questions above. OMIT, where it is an option, is the shortest answer, since taking the material out leaves a shorter text than leaving anything in.

Redundancy, Verbosity, Irrelevance

In the passage above, the wrong (long) answers are either redundant, verbose, or irrelevant. This means that they either make the passage say the same thing twice, force the reader to read more words than necessary, or introduce topics that are off the topic being discussed.

The ACT is very strict about redundancy, verbosity, and irrelevance. Wherever these flaws appear, your first impulse should be to correct them.

REMEMBER THE THREE RULES OF ECONOMY:

REDUNDANCY	• NEVER LET THE TEXT IN A SENTENCE REPEAT ITSELF.
VERBOSITY	• REMEMBER THAT THE BEST WAY TO WRITE SOMETHING IS THE SHORTEST WAY, AS LONG AS IT'S GRAMMATICALLY CORRECT.
IRRELEVANCE	• OMIT THE IDEAS THAT ARE NOT DIRECTLY AND LOGICALLY TIED IN WITH THE PURPOSE OF THE PASSAGE.

When in Doubt . . .

On a real ACT, more than twenty questions—almost one-third of all the English items—test your awareness of redundancy, verbosity, relevance, and similar issues. For these Economy questions the shortest answer is very often correct. So your best bet is: When in doubt, take it out.

Because these issues of writing economy are so important to English questions of all kinds, we've made them the linchpin for our recommended approach to the English test. When approaching English questions, the first question you should ask yourself is: "Does this stuff belong here? Can the passage or sentence work *without* it?"

KAPLAN'S THREE-STEP METHOD

Here's our three-step (or really, three-question) method for ACT English questions.

STEP 1: Ask: "Does this stuff belong here?"

As we've seen, writing economy is very near to the hearts of ACT test makers. So ask yourself: Does the underlined section belong? Is it expressed as succinctly as possible? If the answer is no, choose the answer that gets rid of the stuff that doesn't belong. If the answer is yes, move on to . . .

STEP 2: Ask: "Does this stuff make sense?"

The ACT test makers want simple, easy-to-understand prose. They expect everything to fit together logically. Does the underlined part of the passage make logical sense? If the answer is no, select the choice that turns nonsense into sense. If the answer is yes, go on to . . .

STEP 3: Ask: "Does this stuff sound like English?"

Many grammar errors will sound wrong to your ear. Even the ones that don't will be recognizable to you if you study our Twelve Classic Grammar Errors (in Step 5: ACT English Strategies) and create a "flag list" of the ones you're shaky on. Choose the answer that corrects the error and makes the sentence sound right.

Most ACT English test takers are so worried about grammar and punctuation that they don't think about anything else. That's the wrong mindset. Don't think too much about technical rules. As indicated in the approach above, the first thing is to get rid of unnecessary or irrelevant words. Only after you've decided that the underlined selection *is* concise and relevant do you go on to Steps 2 and 3. This means that you won't necessarily have to go through all three steps on every English question. The answer can come at any point in the three-step method.

SENSE QUESTIONS

Okay, we just saw that the ACT expects you to use words efficiently, and that, in fact, the shortest answer is right remarkably often. But, obviously, the shortest answer is sometimes wrong. What could make it wrong? It may not mean what it says.

Take this example: "Abraham Lincoln's father was a model of hard-working self-sufficiency. He was born in a log cabin he built with his own hands." Well, that's a cute trick, being born in a cabin you built yourself. Presumably the writer means that *Abe* was born in a cabin that his *father* built. But the literal meaning of the example is that the father somehow managed to be born in a cabin that he himself had built.

It's possible, of course, to analyze this example in terms of the rules of apostrophe use and pronoun reference. But that's not practical for the ACT, even for a student who's good at grammar. There isn't time to carefully analyze every question, consider all the rules involved, and decide on an answer. You have to do 75 English questions in only 40 minutes—that's almost two questions per minute.

But there is plenty of time to approach examples like this one in a more pragmatic way. After deciding whether or not the selection in a question is concise and relevant (Step 1 in the three-step method), the next step isn't to remember lots of rules. It's to make sure that the sentence says exactly what it's supposed to *mean*. If not, your job is to fix it.

Make It Make Sense

We at Kaplan have a name for questions that test meaning errors: Sense questions. Once you get the hang of them, these questions can actually be fun. Errors of meaning are often funny once you see them. The following passage gives examples of the most common kinds of Sense questions you'll find on the ACT.

Most people—even those who've never

read Daniel Defoe's *Robinson Crusoe*—

are familiar with the strange story of the

sailor shipwrecked on a far-flung Pacific

island. Relatively few of them, however,

know that Crusoe's <u>story. It was actually</u>
                         1
based on the real-life adventures of a

Scottish seaman, Alexander Selkirk.

Selkirk came to the Pacific as a member

of a 1703 privateering expedition led by a

captain named William Dampier. During

1. A. NO CHANGE
    B. story: was
    C. story, was
    D. story was

the voyage, Selkirk became dissatisfied

with conditions aboard ship. <u>After a bitter</u>
<u>quarrel with his captain, he put Selkirk</u>
<u>ashore</u> on tiny Mas a Tierra, one of the
     2

islands of Juan Fernandez, off the

coast of Chile. Stranded, Selkirk lived

2. F. NO CHANGE
   G. Quarreling with his captain, the boat was put ashore
   H. Having quarreled with his captain, Selkirk was put ashore
   J. Having quarreled with his captain, they put Selkirk ashore
   Ⓕ Ⓖ Ⓗ Ⓙ

there alone—in much the <u>same manner</u>
                              3
<u>as</u> Defoe's Crusoe—until 1709, when
 3
he was finally rescued by another

English privateer.

3. A. NO CHANGE
   B. same manner that
   C. identical manner that
   D. identical way as
   Ⓐ Ⓑ Ⓒ Ⓓ

   Upon his return to England, Selkirk

found himself a <u>celebrity, his</u> strange tale
                       4
had already become the talk of pubs and

coffeehouses throughout the British Isles.

4. F. NO CHANGE
   G. celebrity, but his
   H. celebrity. His
   J. celebrity his
   Ⓕ Ⓖ Ⓗ Ⓙ

The story even reached the ears of Richard Steele, who featured it in his periodical, *The Tatler*. Eventually, <u>he</u>
<u>became</u> the subject of a best-selling
5
book, *A Cruizing Voyage Round the World*, by Woodes Rogers. <u>And while</u> there is
6
some evidence that Defoe, a journalist, may actually have interviewed Selkirk personally, most literary historians believe that it was the reprinting of the Rogers book in 1718 that served as the real stimulus for Defoe's novel.

In *Crusoe*, which <u>has been published</u> in
7
1719, Defoe took substantial liberties with the Selkirk story. For example, while Selkirk's presence on the island was of

5. A. NO CHANGE
   B. Selkirk became
   C. his became
   D. he becomes

6. F. NO CHANGE
   G. But since
   H. And therefore
   J. OMIT the underlined portion and start the sentence with "There."
   Ⓕ Ⓖ Ⓗ Ⓙ

7. A. NO CHANGE
   B. was published
   C. had been published
   D. will have been published
   Ⓐ Ⓑ Ⓒ Ⓓ

course <u>known for many people</u> (certainly
8
everyone in the crew that stranded him

there), no one in the novel is aware of

Crusoe's survival of the wreck and

presence on the island. Moreover, while

Selkirk's exile lasted just six years,

Crusoe's goes on for a much more

dramatic, though less credible, twenty-eight

<u>(over four times as long)</u>. But Defoe's
9
most blatant embellishment of the tale

is the invention of the character of Friday,

for whom there was no counterpart

whatsoever in the real-life story.

   <u>Because of</u> its basis in fact, *Robinson*
10
Crusoe is often regarded as the first

8. F. NO CHANGE
  G. widely known among people
  H. known about many for people
  J. known to many people
   Ⓕ Ⓖ Ⓗ Ⓙ

9. A. NO CHANGE
  B. (much longer)
  C. (a much longer time, of course)
  D. OMIT the underlined portion
   Ⓐ Ⓑ Ⓒ Ⓓ

10. F. NO CHANGE
  G. Despite
  H. Resulting from
  J. As a consequence of
   Ⓕ Ⓖ Ⓗ Ⓙ

major novel in English literature. <u>Still</u>
                                     11
<u>popular today, contemporary audiences</u>
                11
<u>enjoyed the book as well.</u> In fact, two
              11
sequels, in which Crusoe returns to the

island after his rescue, were eventually

<u>published. Though</u> to little acclaim.
        12

Meanwhile, Selkirk himself never <u>gave a</u>
                                     13
<u>hoot about returning</u> to the island that
        13
had made him famous. Legend has it

that he never gave up his eccentric living

habits, spending his last years in a

cave teaching alley cats to dance in his

spare time. One wonders if even Defoe

himself could have invented a more fitting

11. A. NO CHANGE
    B. Still read today,
       Defoe's
       contemporaries
       also enjoyed it.
    C. Viewed by many
       even then as a
       classic, the book
       is still popular to
       this day.
    D. Read widely in its
       day, modern
       people still like the
       book.

    Ⓐ Ⓑ Ⓒ Ⓓ

12. F. NO CHANGE
    G. published, though
    H. published although
    J. published;
       although

    Ⓕ Ⓖ Ⓗ Ⓙ

13. A. NO CHANGE
    B. evinced himself as
       desirous of
       returning
    C. could whip up a
       head of steam to
       return
    D. expressed any
       desire to return

    Ⓐ Ⓑ Ⓒ Ⓓ

end to the bizarre story of his shipwrecked

sailor. 14

Items 14 and 15
pose questions about
the passage as a
whole

14. Considering the tone
and subject matter of
the preceding
paragraphs, is the
last sentence an
appropriate way to
end the essay?
F. Yes, because it is
necessary to shed
some doubt on
Defoe's creativity.
G. Yes, because the
essay is about the
relationship
between the real
Selkirk and
Defoe's
fictionalized
version of him.
H. No, because there
is nothing
"bizarre" about
Selkirk's story as
it is related in the
essay.
J. No, because the
focus of the essay
is more on Selkirk
himself than on
Defoe's
fictionalized
version of him.
Ⓕ Ⓖ Ⓗ Ⓙ

15. This essay would be most appropriate as part of a:
A. scholarly study of eighteenth-century maritime history.
B. study of the geography of the islands off Chile.
C. history of privateering in the Pacific.
D. popular history of English literature.

ANSWERS:

1. D, 2. H, 3. A, 4. H, 5. B, 6. F, 7. B, 8. J, 9. D, 10. G,11. C, 12. G, 13. D, 14. G, 15. D

You may have found these Sense questions harder than the Economy questions. The shortest answers here aren't right nearly as often. But, all other things being equal, the shortest answer is still your best bet. In this case, the correct answers for six out of 15 questions (numbers 1, 3, 7, 9, 10, and 13) were the shortest answers.

On some of the questions in the passage above, you may not have gotten past Step 1 ("Does it belong here?") in Kaplan's three-step method. Question 9, for example, presented material that was clearly redundant. We certainly know that 28 years is longer than six (and if we're really up on our math, we can even figure out that 28 is "more than four times" six), so including any parenthetical aside like the ones given would be unnecessary. Remember, when in doubt, take it out. As we saw earlier, if a question includes an OMIT option, or if some answers are much longer than others, it is usually testing writing economy.

In the rest of the questions in this passage, the answers differ in other ways. They may join or separate sentences, rearrange things, or add words that affect the meaning of the sentences. When the answers are all about the same length, as in most of the questions here, the question is more likely to test sense. Consider the shortest answer first, but don't be as quick to select it and move on. Think about the effect each choice has on the *meaning* of the sentence and pick longer answers if the shortest one doesn't make sense.

GOOD GRAMMAR MAKES GOOD SENSE

The ACT test makers include questions like those in the passage above to test many different rules of writing mechanics. Though it's not *necessary* to think about rules to answer the questions, familiarity with the rules can give you an alternative approach. The more ways you have to think about a question, the more likely you are to find the right answer.

We'll discuss some of these examples in groups based on what they're designed to test. That way we can show you how the basic strategic approach of "make it make sense" can get you the answers without a lot of technical analysis. Let's start with question 1:

. . . Relatively few of them, however,

know that Crusoe's <u>story. It was actually</u>
                             1
based on the real-life adventures of a

Scottish seaman, Alexander Selkirk.

1. A. NO CHANGE
   B. story: was
   C. story, was
   D. story was

If the underlined section for question 1 were left as it is, the second sentence of the passage would be incomplete. It wouldn't make sense. "Relatively few people know that Crusoe's story" what? To make that make sense, you've got to continue the sentence so that it can tell us what it is that few people know about Crusoe's story. The three alternatives all do that, but B introduces a nonsensical colon, while C adds a comma when there's no pause in the sentence. D, however, continues the sentence—adding nothing unnecessary, but making it complete.

Completeness

What question 1 is testing is something we call *completeness*—the requirement that every sentence should consist of an entire thought. Don't just blindly judge the completeness of a sentence by whether it contains a subject and a verb. The alleged sentence—"Relatively few of them, however, know that Crusoe's story."—actually *does* contain a subject and a verb, but it's still not complete. It leaves a thought hanging. Don't leave thoughts hanging on the ACT. The test makers don't like it one bit.

Question 12 also tests this same concept of completeness.

Sentence Structure

Technically, of course, questions 1 and 12 test the broader topic of sentence structure, of which completeness is one part. The "rules" of good sentence structure require that every sentence contain a complete thought. A "sentence" without a complete thought is called a *fragment*. A "sentence" with *too many* complete thoughts (usually connected by commas) is called a *run-on*. That's what we find in question 4:

Upon his return to England, Selkirk found

himself a <u>celebrity, his</u> strange tale had
              4
already become the talk of pubs and

coffeehouses throughout the British Isles.

4. F. NO CHANGE
   G. celebrity, but his
   H. celebrity. His
   J. celebrity his

Here we have two complete thoughts: (1) Selkirk found himself a celebrity upon his return, and (2) his tale was bandied about the pubs and coffeehouses. You can't just run these two complete thoughts together with a comma, as the underlined portion does. And you certainly can't just run them together without a comma or anything else, as choice J does. You can relate the two thoughts with a comma and a linking word (*and, for instance*), but choice G's inclusion of the word *but* makes no sense. It implies a contrast, while the two complete thoughts are actually very similar. Thus, you should create two sentences, one for each thought. That's what correct choice H does.

> **MAKE SURE EVERY SENTENCE CONTAINS AT LEAST ONE, BUT NOT MORE THAN ONE, COMPLETE THOUGHT.**

Modifiers

Question 2 tests modifier problems:

<u>After a bitter quarrel with his captain, he</u>
                  2
<u>put Selkirk ashore</u> on tiny Mas a Tierra,
          2
one of the islands of Juan Fernandez, . . .

2. F. NO CHANGE
   G. Quarreling with his
      captain, the boat
      was put ashore
   H. Having quarreled
      with his captain,
      Selkirk was put
      ashore
   J. Having quarreled
      with his captain,
      they put Selkirk
      ashore

In a well-written sentence, it must be clear exactly what words or phrases are modifying (or referring to) what other words or phrases in the sentence. In the underlined portion here, the clause "after a bitter quarrel with his captain" should modify the pronoun that follows it—*he*. But it doesn't. The *he* who put Selkirk ashore must be the captain, but it can't be the captain who had "a bitter quarrel with his captain." That doesn't make sense (unless the captain quarrels with himself). So put the thing modified next to the thing modifying it. The person who quarreled with his captain was Selkirk—not the boat and not "they," whoever they are—so H is correct.

If you recognized the problem with Question 2 as a "misplaced modifier," that's great. Fantastic, even. But you didn't have to know the technicalities to get the right answer here. You just had to make the sentence make sense.

Question 11, which we won't discuss here, is another question testing modifier placement.

> **MAKE SURE THAT MODIFIERS ARE AS CLOSE AS POSSIBLE TO THE THINGS THEY MODIFY.**

Idiom

Question 3 tests a rather hazy linguistic concept known as *idiom*. The word *idiomatic* refers to language that, well, uses words in the right way. Many words have special rules. If you're a native speaker of the language, you probably picked up many of these rules by ear before your eighth birthday; if you're not a native speaker, you had to learn them one by one.

Stranded, Selkirk lived there alone—in

much the <u>same manner as</u> Defoe's
        3

Crusoe—until 1709, when he was finally

rescued by another . . .

3. A. NO CHANGE
   B. same manner that
   C. identical manner that
   D. identical way as

The sentence as written actually makes perfect sense. Selkirk lived in "much the same manner as" Defoe's Crusoe. The phrase much the same calls for as to complete the comparison between Selkirk's and Crusoe's ways of life. Note how B and C would create completeness problems—in much the same (or identical) manner that Defoe's Crusoe what? Choice D, meanwhile, is just plain unidiomatic. In English, we just don't say "in much the identical way," because the word *identical* is an absolute. You can't be more or partially identical; either you are or aren't identical to something else. But even if you didn't analyze D this carefully, it should have just sounded wrong to your ear. ("Trusting your ear" can be a great way to get correct answers on the English subject test.)

You'll notice that Question 8 tests another idiom problem—the phrase *known to*.

Pronouns

Remember, the object of grammar rules is to make sure that the meaning of language is conveyed clearly. Sometimes, the test will throw you a sentence in which the meaning of a pronoun is unclear. You won't be sure to whom or what the pronoun is referring. That's the kind of problem you were given in Question 5:

The story even reached the ears of

Richard Steele, who featured it in his

periodical, *The Tatler*. Eventually, <u>he</u>
                                       5
<u>became</u> the subject of a best-selling
   5
book . . .

5. A. NO CHANGE
    B. Selkirk became
    C. his became
    D. he becomes

The intended meaning of the pronoun *he* here is as a substitute for "Selkirk." But what's the closest male name to the pronoun? Richard Steele, the publisher of *The Tatler*. That creates an unclear situation. Make it clear! Choice B takes care of the problem by naming Selkirk explicitly. C would create a sense problem. His what became the subject of a book? Meanwhile, D shifts the verb tense into the present, which makes no sense since this book was written over 250 years ago.

> **MAKE SURE IT'S PERFECTLY CLEAR TO WHAT OR TO WHOM ALL PRONOUNS REFER.**

Logic

Structural clues are signal words that an author uses to show where he or she is going in a piece of writing. They show how all of the pieces logically fit together. If the author uses the structural clue *on the other hand*, that means a contrast is coming up. If he or she uses the clue *moreover*, that means that a continuation is coming up—an addition that is more or less in the same vein as what came before.

Many ACT English questions mix up the logic of a piece of writing by giving you the wrong structural clue or other logic word. That's what happened in question 10:

<u>Because of</u> its basis in fact, *Robinson*
        10
Crusoe is often regarded as the first

major novel in English literature.

10. F. NO CHANGE
    G. Despite
    H. Resulting from
    J. As a consequence of

As written, this sentence means that *Crusoe* was regarded as the first major novel because it was based on fact. But that makes no sense. If it was based on fact (which implies nonfiction), that would contradict its being regarded as a novel (which implies fiction). To show that contrast logically, you need a contrast word like *despite*. That's why G is correct here. G makes the sentence make sense.

Question 6 on page 56 also tests logic. *And while* is the right answer, because it first conveys a sense of continuation with the preceding sentence, and then a sense of contrast with the second half of the sentence.

MAKE SURE STRUCTURAL CLUES MAKE LOGICAL SENSE.

Verb Usage

Verbs have an annoying habit of changing form depending on who's doing the action and when he or she is doing it. I *hate* verbs, he *hates* verbs, and we both *have hated* verbs ever since we were kids. Verbs must match their subject and the tense of the surrounding context. Take question 7:

In *Crusoe*, which <u>has been published</u> in
                      7
1719, Defoe took substantial liberties

with the Selkirk story.

7. A. NO CHANGE
   B. was published
   C. had been published
   D. will have been published

The publication of *Robinson Crusoe* is something that took place in 1719—the past, in other words. So the underlined portion, which puts the verb in the present perfect tense, is flawed. Choices C and D, meanwhile, would put the verb into several bizarre tenses. C makes it seem as if publication of the book happened before Defoe took his liberties with the story. But that's nonsensical. The liberties were taken in the writing of the book. D, meanwhile, does strange things with the time sequence. But keep things simple. The book was published in the past; Defoe also took his substantial liberties in more or less the same past. So just use the simple past tense. The book *was published* in 1719, choice B.

> **MAKE SURE ALL VERBS MATCH THEIR SUBJECT AND THE TENSE OF THE SURROUNDING CONTEXT.**

Tone

The passages on the English subject test vary in tone. Some are formal; others are informal. Usually, you'll know which is which without having to think about it. If a passage contains slang, a few exclamation points, and a joke or two, the tone is informal. If it sounds like something a Latin instructor would say, it's probably formal.

Good style requires that the tone of a piece of writing be at the same level throughout. Sometimes the underlined portion might not fit the tone of the rest of the passage. If so, it's up to you to correct it.

Look at question 13:

. . . Meanwhile, Selkirk himself never

<u>gave a hoot about returning</u> to the island
         13
that had made him famous.

13. A. NO CHANGE
   B. evinced himself as desirous of returning
   C. could whip up a head of steam to return
   D. expressed any desire to return

Selkirk "never gave a hoot" about going back? No way! That's slang (and pretty dorky slang, too). It certainly doesn't belong in this passage. This text isn't the most formally written piece of prose in the world, but it's certainly no place for a phrase like "gave a hoot" or (just as bad) "whip up a head of steam" (choice C). B, meanwhile, goes too far in the opposite direction. "Evinced himself as desirous of returning" sounds like something no human being would say. But the rest of the passage sounds human. It makes no sense to shift tonal gears in the middle of a passage. Choose D.

KEEP THE TONE CONSISTENT WITH THE REST OF THE TEXT.

NONSTANDARD-FORMAT ENGLISH QUESTIONS

Some questions ask about the passage as a whole. They're looking for the main point—the gist of the passage—as well as the overall tone and style.

Judging the Passage

Question 14 asks you to judge the passage. Was the last sentence an appropriate ending or not? Most passages will have a well-defined theme, laid out in a logical way. Choose the answer that best continues the logical "flow" of the passage. Some questions on the test will ask you if a passage fits a specified requirement, and often the answer is no.

14. Considering the tone and subject matter of the preceding paragraphs, is the last sentence an appropriate way to end the essay?

   F. Yes, because it is necessary to shed some doubt on Defoe's creativity.

   G. Yes, because the essay is about the relationship between the real Selkirk and Defoe's fictionalized version of him.

   H. No, because there is nothing "bizarre" about Selkirk's story as it is related in the essay.

   J. No, because the focus of the essay is more on Selkirk himself than on Defoe's fictionalized version of him.

Think of the passage as a whole. It's been comparing Selkirk's real life with the one that Defoe made up for Robinson Crusoe. Ending in this way, therefore, with an ironic reference to Defoe as writing a more fitting end to Selkirk's life, is perfectly appropriate. The answer to the question, then, should be yes. F says yes, but gives a nonsensical reason for saying yes. Why is it necessary to shed doubt on Defoe's creativity? Does the author hold a grudge against Defoe? Not that we can tell. So G is the best answer here.

> **MAKE SURE THAT YOUR ANSWER IS IN KEEPING WITH THE LOGICAL "FLOW" OF THE PASSAGE.**

Reading-Type Questions

If you thought question 15 looked like a Reading Comprehension question hiding in the English part of the exam, you were right. As mentioned in ACT Basics, one reason that you should focus on what the passage means, rather than on picky rules of grammar or punctuation, is that the ACT often asks Reading-Type questions.

15. This essay would be most appropriate as part of a:

   A. scholarly study of eighteenth-century maritime history.

   B. study of the geography of the islands off Chile.

   C. history of privateering in the Pacific.

   D. popular history of English literature.

What was this passage principally about? How Defoe's *Robinson Crusoe* was loosely based on the life of a real shipwrecked sailor, Alexander Selkirk. Would that kind of thing belong in a study of geography (choice B)? No; the focus is on the fictionalization of a historical life, not on the physical features of the islands off Chile. The passage isn't principally about privateering or maritime history either, so C and A are wrong, too. This passage is about the relationship of a true story and a famous fictionalized story. And its tone isn't overly scholarly, either. So it probably belongs in a popular history of English literature (choice D).

In this step, we've introduced you to ACT English questions and talked about the first two question types—Economy and Sense questions. In the next step we'll cover what we call Technicality questions, where it really does help to know a handful of grammar rules. But remember that common sense is your best guide on this subject test, and be sure to follow our two keys to success on ACT English: "When in doubt, take it out," and "Make it make sense."

Step 5:
ACT English Strategies

In the first English step, we discussed English questions that hinged mostly on common sense. But there are also some English questions—we call them Technicality questions—that may seem harder because they test for the technical rules of grammar. These require you to correct errors that don't necessarily harm the economy or sense of the sentence. But don't worry. You don't have to be a grammar whiz to get these questions right. Luckily, you can often detect these errors because they "sound funny." Most of the time on the ACT, it's safe to trust your ear.

TRUSTING YOUR EAR

Which of the following "sounds right" and which "sounds funny"?
- Bob doesn't know the value of the house he lives in.
- Bob don't know the value of the house he lives in.

The first sounds a lot better, right? And for many of these questions, all you need to do is to "listen" carefully in this way. You may not know the formal rules of grammar, punctuation, and diction, but you communicate in English every day. You wouldn't be communicating unless you had a decent feel for the rules.

Formal or Informal?

You might have caught an apparent error in *both* of the examples above—ending a sentence with a preposition such as "in." This is undesirable in extremely formal writing. But ACT passages aren't usually that formal. The test makers expect you to have a feel for the level of formality in writing. If the passage is informal, pick informal answers. If the passage is slightly formal (as most ACT passages are), pick slightly formal answers. If the passage is extremely formal, pick extremely formal answers. For example, if the passage starts off with, "You'll just love Bermuda—great beaches, good living . . .," it won't end like this: "and an infinitely fascinating array of flora and fauna which may conceivably exceed, in range and scope, that of any alternative. . . ." That ending is too formal. Pick something like this: "You'll just love Bermuda—great beaches, good living, and a lot of exotic plants and animals."

> **CHOOSE ANSWERS THAT MATCH THE LEVEL OF FORMALITY OF THE ENTIRE PASSAGE.**

Regional and Ethnic Dialects

Although ACT passages differ in level of formality, they all are designed to test "standard" English—the kind used by middle-class people in most of America. Test takers who speak regional or ethnic dialects may therefore find it more difficult to trust their ears on some ACT questions. In much of the South, for instance, it's common to use the word *in* with the word *rate*, like this: "Mortality declined in a rate of almost 2 percent per year." Most English speakers, however, use the word *at* with *rate*, as in: "Mortality declined at a rate of. . . ." Fortunately, ACT questions testing idioms like this are rare. And even if you do speak a "nonstandard" dialect, you probably know what standard English sounds like. The dialect used on most television and radio shows, for example, would be considered "standard."

IF YOU SPEAK A "NONSTANDARD" DIALECT, BE EXTRA CAREFUL WITH QUESTIONS THAT FOCUS ON IDIOMS.

"LISTENING" CAREFULLY

In the following short passage, you may well be able to determine an answer by "listening" carefully to each choice:

Halloween was first celebrated <u>among</u>
                              1
<u>various</u> Celtic tribes in Ireland in the fifth
  1
century B.C. It traditionally took place on

the official last day of summer—

October <u>31, and</u> was named "All Hallows
         2
Eve." It was believed that all persons

who had died during the previous year

returned on this day to select persons

or animals to inhabit for the next twelve

months, until they could <u>pass peaceful</u>
                           3
into the afterlife.

1 A. NO CHANGE
   B. among varied
   C. between the various
   D. between various
   Ⓐ Ⓑ Ⓒ Ⓓ

2. F. NO CHANGE
   G. 31—and
   H. 31. And
   J. 31; and
   Ⓕ Ⓖ Ⓗ Ⓙ

3. A. NO CHANGE
   B. pass peacefully
   C. passed peacefully
   D. be passing peaceful
   Ⓐ Ⓑ Ⓒ Ⓓ

Part Two: The ACT English Test

On All Hallows Eve, the Celts <u>were</u>
<u>dressing</u> up as demons and monsters
    4
to frighten the spirits away, and tried to

make their homes <u>as coldest</u> as possible
                        5
to prevent any stray ghosts from crossing

their thresholds. Late at night, the

townspeople typically gathered outside the

village, where a druidic priest would light a

huge bonfire to frighten away ghosts and

to honor the sun god for the past

summer's harvest. Any villager <u>whom was</u>
                                    6
suspected of being possessed would be

captured, after which <u>they</u> might be
                        7
sacrificed in the bonfire as a warning to

other spirits seeking to possess the

living.

When the Romans invaded the British

Isles, they adopted Celtic—not Saxon—

4. F. NO CHANGE
   G. were dressed
   H. dressed
   J. are dressed
   Ⓕ Ⓖ Ⓗ Ⓙ

5. A. NO CHANGE
   B. colder
   C. coldest
   D. as cold
   Ⓐ Ⓑ Ⓒ Ⓓ

6. F. NO CHANGE
   G. whom were
   H. who was
   J. who were
   Ⓕ Ⓖ Ⓗ Ⓙ

7. A. NO CHANGE
   B. it
   C. he or she
   D. those
   Ⓐ Ⓑ Ⓒ Ⓓ

Halloween rituals, but outlawed human

sacrifice in A.D. 61. Instead, they used

effigies for their sacrifices. In time, as

belief in spirit possession waned,
    8
Halloween rituals lost their serious aspect

and had been instead performed for
    9
amusement.

   Irish immigrants, fleeing from the potato

famine in the 1840s, brought there
               10
Halloween customs to the United States.

In New England, Halloween became a night

of costumes and practical jokes. Some

favorite pranks included unhinging front
           11
gates and overturning outhouses. The

Irish also introduced the custom of carving

jack-o'-lanterns. The ancient Celts

probably began the tradition by hollowing

out a large turnip, carving its face, and

8. F. NO CHANGE
   G. belief for
   H. believing about
   J. belief of
       Ⓕ Ⓖ Ⓗ Ⓙ

9. A. NO CHANGE
   B. having been
   C. have been
   D. were
       Ⓐ Ⓑ Ⓒ Ⓓ

10. F. NO CHANGE
   G. brought they're
   H. brought their
   J. their brought-in
       Ⓕ Ⓖ Ⓗ Ⓙ

11. A. NO CHANGE
   B. include unhinging
   C. had included unhinged
   D. includes unhinged
       Ⓐ Ⓑ Ⓒ Ⓓ

lighting it from inside with a candle. Since

there were <u>far less</u> turnips in New
       12
England than in Ireland, the Irish

immigrants were forced to settle for

pumpkins.

    Gradually, Halloween celebrations

spread to other regions of the United

States. Halloween has been a popular

holiday ever since, <u>although these days</u>
             13
<u>it's</u> principal celebrants are children <u>rather</u>
13   14
<u>than</u> adults.
14

12. F. NO CHANGE
    G. lots less
    H. not as much
    J. far fewer

        F G H J

13. A. NO CHANGE
    B. although these
       days its
    C. while now it's
    D. while not it is

        A B C D

14. F. NO CHANGE
    G. rather then
    H. rather
    J. else then

        F G H J

ANSWERS

ANSWER		PROBLEM
1.	A	*among/between* distinction (see Classic Grammar Error 11 below)
2.	G	commas and dashes mixed (see Classic Grammar Error 2 below)
3.	B	use of adjectives and adverbs (see Classic Grammar Error 6 below)
4.	H	unnecessary *-ing* ending
5.	D	comparative/superlative (see Classic Grammar Error 10 below)

6.	H	*who/whom* confusion
7.	C	pronoun usage error (see Classic Grammar Error 1 below)
8.	F	preposition usage
9.	D	tense problem with *to be*
10.	H	*they're/there/their* mixup (see Classic Grammar Error 8 below)
11.	A	verb tense usage (see Classic Grammar Error 9 below)
12.	J	*less/fewer* confusion (see Classic Grammar Error 12 below)
13.	B	*it's/its* confusion (see Classic Grammar Error 7 below)
14.	F	*then/than* usage

TWELVE CLASSIC GRAMMAR ERRORS

Many students could rely almost exclusively on their ear to correct many of the errors above. But there are a few English questions on the ACT that contain errors your ear probably won't or can't catch. If you have a good ear for English, there may be only a handful of such questions on the test. If not, there may be many more. For these, you'll have to think about the rules more formally. But fortunately, only a small number of rules are typically involved, and we'll discuss the most common ones in this step. Even more fortunately, most of the technicalities tested on the ACT boil down to one general principal: *Make it all match.*

The rest of this step is designed to help you build your own "flag list" of common errors on the ACT that your ear might not catch. Consider each classic error. If it seems like common sense to you (or, better, if the error just *sounds* like bad English to you, while the correction *sounds* like good English), you probably don't have to add it to your flag list. If, on the other hand, the error doesn't seem obvious, add it to your list.

As we'll see, making things match works in two ways. Some rules force you to match one part of the sentence with another. Other rules force you to match the right word or word form with the meaning intended.

ERROR 1: *IT* AND *THEY* (SINGULARS AND PLURALS)

The "matching" rule tested most on the ACT is this: Singular nouns must match with singular verbs and pronouns, and plural nouns must match with plural verbs and pronouns. The most common error in this area involves the use of the word *they*. It's plural, but in everyday speech, we incorrectly use it as singular.

SENTENCE: "If a student won't study, they won't do well."

PROBLEM: A *student* (singular) and *they* (plural) don't match.

CORRECTION: "If students won't study, they won't do well." "If a student won't study, he (or she) won't do well."

> **WATCH FOR SUBJECT-VERB AND NOUN-PRONOUN AGREEMENT.**

ERROR 2: COMMAS OR DASHES (PARENTHETICAL PHRASES)

One rule of punctuation is tested far more often than any other on the ACT. Parenthetical phrases must *begin* and *end* with the same punctuation mark. Such phrases can be recognized because without them, the sentence would still be complete. For instance: "Bob, on his way to the store, saw a large lizard in the street." If you dropped the phrase "on his way to the store," the sentence would still be complete. Thus, this phrase is parenthetical. It could be marked off with commas, parentheses, or dashes. But the same mark is needed at both ends of the phrase.

SENTENCE:	"Bob—on his way to the store, saw a lizard."
PROBLEM:	The parenthetical phrase starts with a dash but finishes with a comma.
CORRECTION:	"Bob, on his way to the store, saw a lizard."

MAKE SURE PARENTHETICAL PHRASES BEGIN AND END WITH THE SAME PUNCTUATION MARK.

ERROR 3: RUN-ONS AND COMMA SPLICES

The ACT test makers expect you to understand what makes a sentence and what doesn't. You can't combine two sentences into one with a comma (though you can with a semicolon or conjunction).

SENTENCE:	"Ed's a slacker, Sara isn't."
PROBLEM:	Two sentences are spliced together with a comma.
CORRECTION:	"Ed's a slacker, but Sara isn't."
	"Ed's a slacker; Sara isn't."
	"Ed, unlike Sara, is a slacker."

Usually, only one thing should happen in each sentence. There should be one "major event." There are only a few ways to put more than one event in a sentence. One way is to connect the sentences with a comma and a conjunction (a word such as *and* or *but*), as in the first correction. Or, as in the second, a semicolon can stand in for such a word. The other way is to "subordinate" one event to the other in a clause, as in the third correction.

ERROR 4: FRAGMENTS

This rule goes hand-in-hand with the one above. A "fragment" is writing that could be a subordinate part of a sentence, but not a whole sentence itself.

SENTENCE: "Emily listened to music. While she studied."

PROBLEM: "She studied" would be a sentence, but while makes this a fragment.

CORRECTION: "Emily listened to music while she studied."

LOOK OUT FOR SENTENCE FRAGMENTS AND RUN-ON SENTENCES.

ERROR 5: MISUNDERSTOOD PUNCTUATION MARKS

The test makers don't test tricky rules of punctuation. But they do expect you to know what the punctuation marks mean and to match their use to their meanings. Here are some common ones:

- Period (.)—Means "full stop" or "end of sentence."
- Question mark (?)—Serves the same purpose, but for questions.
- Exclamation mark (!)—Can be used instead of a period, but is generally inappropriate for all but very informal writing because it indicates extreme emotion.
- Comma (,)—Represents a pause. In many cases a comma is optional. But never use a comma where a pause would be confusing, as in: "I want to go, to the, store."
- Semicolon (;)—Used to separate two complete but closely related thoughts.
- Colon (:)—Works like an "=" sign, connecting two equivalent things. Colons are usually used to begin a list.

• Dash (—)—Can be used for any kind of pause, usually a long one or one indicating a significant shift in thought.

ERROR 6: -LY ENDINGS (ADVERBS AND ADJECTIVES)

The test makers expect you to understand the difference between adverbs (the -ly words) and adjectives. The two are similar because they're both modifiers. They modify, or refer to, or describe, another word or phrase in the sentence. But nouns and pronouns must be modified by *adjectives*, while other words, especially verbs and adjectives themselves, must be modified by *adverbs*.

SENTENCE: "Anna is an extreme gifted child, and she speaks beautiful, too."

PROBLEM: *Extreme* and *beautiful* are adjectives, but they're supposed to modify an adjective (*gifted*) and a verb (*speaks*) here, so they should be adverbs.

CORRECTION: "Anna is an extremely gifted child, and she speaks beautifully, too."

NOUNS AND PRONOUNS ARE MODIFIED BY ADJECTIVES.
VERBS AND ADJECTIVES ARE MODIFIED BY ADVERBS.

ERROR 7: *ITS* AND *IT'S* (APOSTROPHE USE)

Probably the trickiest rule is the proper use of apostrophes. Apostrophes are used primarily for two purposes: possessives and contractions. When you make a noun (not a pronoun) possessive by adding an *s*, you use an apostrophe. For example: *Bob's, the water's, a noodle's.* But you *never* use an apostrophe to make a pronoun possessive—pronouns have special possessive forms. You would never write *her's.* (One exception is the pronoun *one,* as in, "One's hand is attached to one's wrist.") When you run two words together to form a single word, to form a contraction, you use an apostrophe to join them. For example: *I'm, he's, they're.*

Apostrophes also have a few unusual uses, but luckily they're almost never tested on the ACT. So, master the basics and you'll be in good shape.

The most common apostrophe issue on the ACT is usage of *its* and *it's.* These two words follow the same rule as do *his* and *he's.* Both *its* and *his* are possessive pronouns—so they have no apostrophes. Both *it's* and *he's* are contractions—so they do have apostrophes.

SENTENCE: "The company claims its illegal to use it's name that way."

PROBLEM: *It's* is a contraction of *it is; its* is the possessive form of *it.*

CORRECTION: "The company claims it's illegal to use its name that way."

> *IT'S* IS A CONTRACTION FOR *IT IS*, WHILE *ITS* SHOWS
> POSSESSION.

ERROR 8: *THERE, THEIR, THEY'RE* AND *ARE, OUR* (PROPER WORD USAGE)

Some students confuse the words *there, their,* and *they're.* Contractions use apostrophes—so *they're* is the contraction for *they are.* You can tell when to use *there* because it's spelled like *here,* and the words *here* and *there* both indicate location. *Their* means "of or belonging to them." You'll just have to remember that one the old-fashioned way.

Students also frequently confuse the words *are* (a verb) and *our* (a possessive). You can remember that *our* is spelled like *your,* another (less confusing) possessive.

> **LEARN TO DISTINGUISH THE WORDS *THERE, THEIR,* AND *THEY'RE*.**

ERROR 9: *SANG, SUNG, BRANG, BRUNG,* ETC. (VERB FORMS)

When you have to consider different forms of the same verb (for example, *live, lives, lived*), ask yourself who did it and when did they do it? We would say, "I now live" but "he now lives." In these sentences, the *who* is different—and so the verb changes. Similarly, we would say, "I now live" but "I lived in the past." In these sentences, the *when* is different—so the verb changes.

Most verbs are "regular" in this way. You add *s* when the subject is *he, she,* or *it* and the time is now (present tense). You add *d* for times in the past. For times in the future, or several steps back in the past, there are no special endings; you use the words *will, will have, have,* and *had.* I *will* live. I *will have* lived for 25 years by the time the next century begins. I *had* lived in Nebraska, but we moved. I *have* lived in Indiana since then.

But a few verbs are irregular. They have special forms. For example, we say *sang* rather than *singed* and *have sung* rather than *have singed* or *have sang.* Each of these verbs must be learned separately.

One irregular verb commonly tested on the ACT is *bring.*

SENTENCE: "I've brung my umbrella to work."

PROBLEM: *Brang* and *brung* aren't used in standard English.

CORRECTION: "I've brought my umbrella to work."

ERROR 10: *-ER* AND *-EST*, *MORE* AND *MOST* (COMPARATIVES AND SUPERLATIVES)

Whenever you see the endings *-er* or *-est*, or the words *more* or *most*, double-check to make sure they're used logically. Words with *-er* or with *more* should be used to compare only two things. If there are more than two things involved, use *-est* or *most*.

SENTENCE: "Bob is the fastest of the two runners."

PROBLEM: The comparison is between just two things, so the *-est* ending is inappropriate.

CORRECTION: "Bob is the faster of the two runners."

Don't use the words *more* or *most* if you can use the *-er* and *-est* endings instead. Say, "I think vanilla is tastier than chocolate," not "I think vanilla is more tasty than chocolate." Never use both *more* or *most* and an *est/er* ending. Don't say, "Of the five flavors of frozen yogurt I've eaten, strawberry delight is the most tastiest." Just say it's "the tastiest."

ERROR 11: CONFUSING *BETWEEN* AND *AMONG*

As a rule of thumb, use the word *between* only when there are two things involved, or when comparisons in a larger group are made between pairs of things. When there are more than two things, or an unknown number of things, use *among*.

SENTENCES: "I will walk among the two halves of the class."

                "I will walk between the many students in class."

PROBLEM: Use *between* for two things; *among* for more than two.

CORRECTION: "I will walk between the two halves of the class."

"I will walk among the many students in class."

ERROR 12: CONFUSING *LESS* AND *FEWER*

Make sure that you use the word *less* only for uncountable things. When things can be counted, they are *fewer*.

SENTENCE: "I have fewer water than I thought, so I can fill less buckets."

PROBLEM: You can count buckets; you can't count water.

CORRECTION: "I have less water than I thought, so I can fill fewer buckets."

HINT: People are always countable, so you should always use fewer when writing about them.

USE *FEWER* WITH COUNTABLE NOUNS, AND *LESS* WITH UNCOUNTABLE NOUNS.

THE ACT MATH TEST

STEP 6:
CLASSIC MATH STRATEGIES

All that matters on the ACT is correct answers. Your goal on the math subject test is to get as many correct answers as you can in 60 minutes. It doesn't matter what you do (short of cheating, naturally) to get those correct answers. What matters is using quick methods that get you a solid number of correct answers.

> **WORRY ABOUT RIGHT ANSWERS, NOT "RIGHT" WAYS OF SOLVING PROBLEMS.**

QUESTION BREAKDOWN

Each ACT Math subject test includes the following:
- 24 prealgebra and elementary algebra questions
- 10 intermediate algebra questions
- 8 coordinate geometry questions
- 14 plane geometry questions
- 4 trigonometry questions

Nobody needs to get all 60 questions right. The average ACT student gets fewer than half of the math questions right! You need only about 40 correct answers to get your math score over 25—just two right out of every three questions gets you a great score. So if, for instance, you're hopeless in trigonometry, just forget it!

> **IF YOU DON'T KNOW YOUR TRIG BY NOW, YOU'RE PROBABLY BETTER OFF JUST SKIPPING THE FOUR TRIGONOMETRY QUESTIONS ON YOUR MATH SUBJECT TEST.**

As you can see, you get only four trigonometry questions on any test. Those are four points you can sacrifice at this late date—so that you can focus on things such as algebra questions, which account for a much larger portion of the Math subject test.

BE A THINKER—NOT A NUMBER CRUNCHER

One reason you're given limited time for the Math subject test is that the ACT is testing your ability to think, not your willingness to do a lot of mindless calculations. They're looking for creative thinkers, not human calculators. So, one of your guiding principles for ACT math should be: Work less, but work smarter.

If you want to get the best score you can, you need to be always on the lookout for quicker ways to solve problems. Here's an example that could take a lot more time than it needs to.

1. When $\frac{4}{11}$ is converted to a decimal, the 50th digit after the decimal point is

   A. 2

   B. 3

   C. 4

   D. 5

   E. 6

It seems that when you convert $\frac{4}{11}$ to a decimal, there are at least 50 digits after the decimal point. The question asks for the 50th. One way to answer this question would be to divide 11 into 4, carrying the division out to 50 decimal places. That method would work, but it would take forever. It's not worth spending that much time on one question.

No ACT math question should take more than a minute, if you know what you're doing. There has to be a faster way to solve this problem. There must be some kind of pattern you can take advantage of. And what kind of pattern might there be with a decimal? How about a repeating decimal!

In fact, that's exactly what you have here. The decimal equivalent of $\frac{4}{11}$ is a repeating decimal:

$$\frac{4}{11} = .3636363636....$$

The first, third, fifth, seventh, and ninth digits are each 3. The second, fourth, sixth, eighth, and tenth digits are each 6. To put it simply, odd-numbered digits are 3s and even-numbered digits are 6s. The fiftieth digit is an even-numbered digit, so it's a 6 and the answer is E.

What looked at first glance like a "fractions-and-decimals" problem turned out to be something of an "odds-and-evens" problem.

If you don't use creative shortcuts on problems like this one, you'll get bogged down, you'll run out of time, and you won't get a lot of questions right.

Question 1 demonstrates how the ACT designs problems to reward clever thinking and to punish students who blindly "go through the motions."

But how do you get yourself into a creative mindset on the Math subtest? For one thing, you have to take the time to understand thoroughly each problem you decide to work on. Most students are so nervous about time that they skim each math problem and almost immediately start computing with their pencils. But that's the wrong way of thinking. Sometimes on the ACT, you have to take time to save time. A few extra moments spent understanding a math problem can save many extra moments of computation or other drudgery.

> **TAKE TIME TO LOOK FOR SHORTCUTS THAT WILL SAVE TIME IN THE LONG RUN.**

KAPLAN'S THREE-STEP METHOD FOR ACT MATH

At Kaplan, we've developed this take-time-to-save-time philosophy into a three-step method for solving ACT math problems. The method is designed to help you find the fast, inventive solutions that the ACT rewards. The steps are:

STEP 1: Understand

Focus first on the question stem (the part before the answer choices) and make sure you understand the problem. Sometimes you'll want to read the stem twice, or rephrase it in a way you can better understand. Think to yourself: "What kind of problem is this? What am I looking for? What am I given?" Don't pay too much attention to the answer choices yet, though you may want to give them a quick glance just to see what form they're in.

STEP 2: Analyze

Think for a moment and decide on a plan of attack. Don't start crunching numbers until you've given the problem a little thought. "What's a quick and reliable way to find the correct answer?" Look for patterns and shortcuts, using common sense and your knowledge of the test to find the creative solutions that will get you more right answers in less time. Try to solve the problem without focusing on the answer choices.

STEP 3: Select

Once you get an answer—or once you get stuck—check the answer choices. If you got an answer and it's listed as one of the choices, chances are it's right; fill in the appropriate bubble and move on. But if you didn't get an answer, narrow down the choices as best you can, by a process of elimination, and then guess.

Each of these steps can happen in a matter of seconds. And it may not always be clear when you've finished with one step and moved on to the next. Sometimes you'll know how to attack a problem the instant you read and understand it.

Let's look at a specific problem.

2. If the sum of five consecutive even integers is equal to their product, what is the greatest of the five integers?

   F. 4

   G. 10

   H. 14

   J. 16

   K. 20

Step 1: Understand

Before you can begin to solve this problem, you have to figure out what it's asking, and to do that you need to know the meanings of sum, product, consecutive, even, and integer. Put the question stem into words you can understand. What it's really saying is that when you add up these five consecutive even integers you get the same thing as when you multiply them.

Step 2: Analyze

How are we going to figure out what these five numbers are? We could set up an equation:

$$x + (x - 2) + (x - 4) + (x - 6) + (x - 8) = x(x - 2)(x - 4)(x - 6)(x - 8)$$

But there's no way you'll have time to solve an equation like this! So don't even try. Come up with a better way.

Let's stop and think logically about this. When we think about sums and products, it's natural to think mostly of positive integers. With positive integers, we would generally expect the product to be *greater* than the sum.

But what about negative integers? Hmm. Well, the sum of five negatives is negative, and the product of five negatives is also negative, and generally the product will be "more negative" than the sum, so with negative integers the product will be *less* than the sum.

So when will the product and sum be the same? How about right at the boundary between positive and negative—that is, around 0? The five consecutive even integers with equal product and sum are −4, −2, 0, 2, and 4.

$(-4) \times (-2) \times 0 \times 2 \times 4 = (-4) + (-2) + 0 + 2 + 4$

The product and sum are both 0. Ha! We've done it!

Step 3: Select

The question asks for the greatest of the five integers, which is 4, choice F.

CLARIFY TO YOURSELF WHAT A MATH QUESTION IS ASKING.

ow let's look at a case in which the method of solution is not so
vious.

4. What is the greatest of the numbers 1^{50}, 50^1, 2^{25}, 25^2, 4^{10} ?

    F. 1^{50}

    G. 50^1

    H. 2^{25}

    J. 25^2

    K. 4^{10}

Step 1: Understand

It's not hard to figure out what the question's asking: Which of five numbers is the greatest? But the five numbers are all written as powers, some of which we don't have time to calculate. Yikes! How are we going to compare them?

Step 2: Analyze

If all the powers had the same base or the same exponent, or if they could all be rewritten with a common base or exponent, we could compare all five at once. As it is, though, we should take two at a time.

Compare 1^{50} and 50^1 to start. $1^{50} = 1$, while $50^1 = 50$, so there's no way choice F could be the biggest.

Next compare 50^1 and 2^{25} We don't have time to calculate 2^{25}, but we can see that it doesn't take anywhere near 25 factors of 2 to get over 50. In fact, 2^6 is 64, already more than 50, so 2^{25} is much, much more than 50. That eliminates G.

Choice J, 25^2, doesn't take too long to calculate: $25 \times 25 = 625$. How does that compare to 2^{25}? Once again, with a little thought, we realize that it doesn't take 25 factors of 2 to get over 625. That eliminates J.

The last comparison is easy because choice K, 4^{10}, can be rewritten as $(2^2)^{10} = 2^{20}$, in that form clearly less than 2^{25}. That eliminates K.

Step 3: Select

So the answer is H.

DEFINITION ALERT

You've probably encountered every math term that appears on the ACT sometime in high school, but you may not remember what each one means. Here are a few small but important technicalities that you may have forgotten:

- **"Integers" include 0 and negative whole numbers.**
  If a question says, "x and y are integers," it's not ruling out numbers like 0 and -1.
- **"Evens and odds" include 0 and negative whole numbers.**
  0 and -2 are even numbers. -1 is an odd number.
- **"Prime numbers" do not include 1.**
  The technical definition of a prime number is, "a positive integer with exactly two distinct positive integer factors."

$$(-4) \times (-2) \times 0 \times 2 \times 4 = (-4) + (-2) + 0 + 2 + 4$$

The product and sum are both 0. Ha! We've done it!

Step 3: Select

The question asks for the greatest of the five integers, which is 4, choice F.

CLARIFY TO YOURSELF WHAT A MATH QUESTION IS ASKING.

Now let's look at a case in which the method of solution is not so obvious.

4.   What is the greatest of the numbers 1^{50}, 50^1, 2^{25}, 25^2, 4^{10} ?

    F. 1^{50}

    G. 50^1

    H. 2^{25}

    J. 25^2

    K. 4^{10}

Step 1: Understand

It's not hard to figure out what the question's asking: Which of five numbers is the greatest? But the five numbers are all written as powers, some of which we don't have time to calculate. Yikes! How are we going to compare them?

Step 2: Analyze

If all the powers had the same base or the same exponent, or if they could all be rewritten with a common base or exponent, we could compare all five at once. As it is, though, we should take two at a time.

since you know a second visit later won't help, you might as well go ahead and guess.

It can be harder to decide when to skip a question if you understand it, but then get stuck in Step 2: "Analyze." Suppose you just don't see how to solve it. Don't give up too quickly. Sometimes it takes a half-minute or so before you see the light. But don't get bogged down, either. Never spend more than a minute on a question the first time through. Be prepared to leave a question and come back to it later. Often, on the second try, you'll see something you didn't see earlier.

Eventually, you're going to grid in answer choices for all the questions, even the ones you don't understand. The first time through, though, concentrate on the questions you understand.

WHAT TO DO WHEN YOU'RE STUCK

Let's say you're on your second pass. You've done some good work on a particular question, but you just can't get an answer. What you *don't* want to do is stall and waste time. What you *do* want to do is take your best shot at the question and move on. Guesstimating and eyeballing are two handy methods for doing just that.

Estimates and Guesstimates

Sometimes when you understand a problem but can't figure out how to solve it, you can at least get a general idea of how big the answer is—what is sometimes called a "ballpark estimate," or "guesstimate." You may not know whether you are looking at something the size of an African elephant or the size of an Indian elephant, but you may be pretty sure it isn't the size of a mouse and it isn't the size of a battleship.

Here's a question that's not hard to understand but is hard to solve if you don't remember the rules for simplifying and adding radicals:

5. $\dfrac{\sqrt{32} + \sqrt{24}}{\sqrt{8}} = ?$

    A. $\sqrt{7}$

    B. $\sqrt{2} + \sqrt{3}$

    C. $2 + \sqrt{3}$

    D. $\sqrt{2} + 3$

    E. 7

Step 1: Understand

The question wants you to simplify the given expression, which includes three radicals. In other words, turn the radicals into numbers you can use, then work out the fraction.

Step 2: Analyze

The best way to solve this problem would be to apply the rules of radicals—but what if you don't remember them? Don't give up; you can still guesstimate. In the question stem, the numbers under the radicals are not too far away from perfect squares. You could round $\sqrt{32}$ off to $\sqrt{36}$, which is 6. You could round $\sqrt{24}$ to $\sqrt{25}$, which is 5. And you could round $\sqrt{8}$ off to $\sqrt{9}$, which is 3. So the expression is now $\dfrac{6 + 5}{3}$, which is $3\frac{2}{3}$. That's just a guesstimate, of course—the actual value might be something a bit less or a bit more than that.

Step 3: Select

Now look at the answer choices. Choice A, $\sqrt{7}$, is less than 3, so it's

2 is prime because it has exactly two positive factors: 1 and 2. 4 is not prime because it has three positive factors (1, 2, and 4) —too many! And 1 is not prime because it has only one positive factor (1)—too few!

- **"Remainders" are integers.**
  If a question asks for the remainder when 15 is divided by 2, don't say, "15 divided by 2 is 7.5, so the remainder is .5." What you should say is: "15 divided by 2 is 7 with a remainder of 1."

- **The $\sqrt{\ }$ symbol represents the positive square root only.**
  The equation $x^2 = 9$ has two solutions: 3 and –3. But when you see $\sqrt{9}$, it means positive 3 only.

- **"Rectangles" include squares.**
  A rectangle is a four-sided figure with four right angles, whether or not the length and width are the same. When a question refers to "rectangle *ABCD*," it's not ruling out a square.

LEARN THE SMALL BUT IMPORTANT TECHNICALITIES THAT CAN HELP YOU EARN POINTS.

KAPLAN'S TWO-PASS PLAN FOR ACT MATH

We recommend that you plan two "passes" through the Math subtest.

- **First Pass:** Examine each problem in order. Do every problem you understand. Don't skip too hastily— sometimes it takes a few seconds of thought to see how to do something—but don't get bogged down. Never spend more than a minute on any question in the first pass. This first pass should take about 45 minutes.

- **Second Pass:** Use the last 15 minutes to go back to the questions that stumped you the first time. Sometimes a fresh second look is all you need, and you might suddenly see what to do. In most cases, though, you'll still be stumped by the question stem, so it's time to give the answer choices a try. Work by process of elimination, and guess.

Don't plan on visiting a question a third time; it's inefficient to go back and forth that much. Always grid in an answer choice on the second pass, every question should be answered.

Don't worry if you don't work on every question in the section. The average ACT test taker gets fewer than half of the problems right. You can score in the top quarter of all ACT test takers if you can do just half of the problems on the test, get every single one of them right, and guess blindly on the other half. If you did just *one-third* of the problems and got every one right, then guessed blindly on the other forty problems, you would still earn an average score.

KNOW WHEN TO PASS ON A QUESTION

At any time during the three-step problem-solving process you could choose to cut bait and skip the question. Almost everyone should skip at least some questions the first time through. (But remember, don't leave these questions blank! Always go back and guess if you have to.)

If you know your own strengths and weaknesses, you can some-times choose to skip a question while still in Step 1: "Understand." For example, suppose you never studied trigonometry—maybe you think that a secant is something that sailors sing while climbing up the yardarms. Well, the ACT includes four trigonometry questions, and it's not hard to spot them. Why not pass on such questions? You don't need those four measly questions to get a great score. And

too small. Choice B, $\sqrt{2} + \sqrt{3}$, is about $1.4 + 1.7$, or just barely more than 3, so it seems a little small, too. Choice C, $2 + \sqrt{3}$, is about $2 + 1.7$, or about 3.7—that's very close to our guesstimate! We still have to check the other choices. Choice D, $\sqrt{2} + 3$, is about $1.4 + 3$, or 4.4—too big. And choice E, 7, is obviously way too big. Looks like our best bet is C—and C, in fact, is the correct answer.

IT PAYS TO LEARN THE APPROXIMATE VALUE OF THESE THREE IRRATIONAL NUMBERS:

$\sqrt{2} \approx 1.4$

$\sqrt{3} \approx 1.7$

$\pi \approx 3.14$

Eyeballing

There is another simple but powerful strategy that should give you at least a 50-50 chance on almost every diagram question: When in doubt, use your eyes. Trust common sense and careful thinking; don't worry if you've forgotten most of the geometry you ever knew. For almost half of all diagram questions you can get a reasonable answer without solving anything. Just eyeball it.

The math directions say, "Illustrative figures are NOT necessarily drawn to scale," but in fact they almost always are. You're never really supposed to just eyeball the figure, but it makes a lot more sense than random guessing. Occasionally eyeballing can narrow the choices down to one likely candidate.

Here's a difficult geometry question that you might just decide to eyeball:

6. In the figure below, points *A*, *B*, and *C* lie on a circle centered at *O*. Triangle *AOC* is equilateral, and the length of *OC* is 3 inches. What is the length, in inches, of arc *ABC* ?

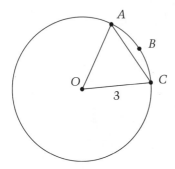

F. 3

G. π

H. 2π

J. 3π

K. 6π

Step 1: Understand

There's an "equilateral" triangle that connects the center and two points on the circumference of a circle. We're looking for the length of the arc that goes from *A* to *C*.

Step 2: Analyze

What you're "supposed" to do to answer this question is recall and apply the formula for the length of an arc. But suppose you don't remember that formula (most people don't). Should you give up and take a wild guess?

No. You can eyeball it. If you understand the question well enough to realize that "equilateral" means that all sides are equal, then you know immediately that side $\overline{AC}$ is 3 inches long. Now look at arc *ABC* compared to side $\overline{AC}$. Suppose you were an ant, and you had to walk from *A* to *C*. If you walked along line segment $\overline{AC}$, it would be a 3-inch trip. About how long a walk would it be along arc *ABC* ? Clearly more, but not much more, than 3 inches.

Step 3: Select

Now look at the answer choices. Choice F, 3, is no good; we know the arc is more than 3 inches. All the other choices are in terms of π. Just think of π as "a bit more than 3," and you will quickly see that only one answer choice is in the right ballpark. Choice G, π, would be "a bit more than 3," which sounds pretty good. Choice H, 2π, would be "something more than 6"—way too big. Choices J and K are even bigger. It looks like the answer has to be G—and it is.

This is a pretty hard question. Not many ACT students would be able to solve it the textbook way. If you did, great! That's the way to do it if you know how. Solving the problem is always more reliable than eyeballing.

But when you don't know how to solve a diagram problem, or if you think it would take forever to get an answer, eyeballing and eliminating answer choices sure beat wild guessing. Sometimes, as with question 6, you might even be able to narrow down the choices to the one that's probably correct.

**EYEBALL A GEOMETRY PROBLEM IF YOU DON'T HAVE
THE TIME OR KNOWLEDGE TO SOLVE IT.**

This step has introduced you to the methods for success on ACT Math. In the next math step we'll give you some advice about calculator use, and in the final two math steps, we'll talk about specific strategies for the two major areas of ACT Math—algebra and geometry.

KAPLAN

Step 7:
Calculator Techniques

Students are permitted to use calculators on the Math section of the ACT. The good news for noncalculator users is that you never *absolutely need* to use a calculator to answer the questions on the ACT. No math question will require messy or tedious calculations. But while the calculator can't answer questions for you, it can keep you from making computational errors on questions you know how to solve. The bad news, however, is that a calculator can actually cost you time if you overuse it. Take a look at this example:

1. The sum of all the integers from 1 to 44, inclusive, is subtracted from the sum of all the integers from 7 to 50, inclusive. What is the result?

   A.   6

   B.   44

   C.   50

   D. 264

   E. 300

You could . . . add all the integers from 1 through 44, and then all the integers from 7 through 50, and then subtract the first sum from the second. And then punch all the numbers into the calculator. And then hope you didn't hit any wrong buttons.

IF A PROBLEM SEEMS TO INVOLVE A LOT OF CALCULATION, LOOK FOR A QUICKER WAY.

But that's the long way . . . and the wrong way. That way involves hitting over 250 keys on your calculator. It'll take too long, and you're too likely to make a mistake. The amount of computation involved in solving this problem tells you that there must be an easier way. Remember, no ACT problem absolutely requires the use of a calculator.

THE RIGHT WAY—THINK FIRST

Let's look at that problem again:

1. The sum of all the integers from 1 to 44, inclusive, is subtracted from the sum of all the integers from 7 to 50, inclusive. What is the result?

   A. 6

   B. 44

   C. 50

   D. 264

   E. 300

A calculator *can* help you on this question, but you have to think first. Both sums contain the same number of consecutive integers, and each integer in the first sum has a corresponding integer 6 greater than it in the second sum. Here's the scratchwork:

1	7
+2	+8
+3	+9
.	.
.	.
.	.
+42	+48
+43	+49
+44	+50

This means there are 44 pairs of integers that are each 6 apart. So the total difference between the two sums will be the difference between each pair of integers, times the number of pairs. Now you can pull out your calculator, punch "$6 \times 44 =$" and get the correct answer of 264 with little or no time wasted. Mark (D) in your test booklet and move on.

Here's another way to solve it. Both sets of integers contain the integers 7 through 44 inclusive. Think of $7 + 8 + 9 + 10 + \ldots + 50$ as $(7 + 8 + 9 + 10 + \ldots + 44) + (45 + 46 + 47 + 48 + 49 + 50)$. Now think of $1 + 2 + 3 + 4 + \ldots + 44$ as $(1 + 2 + 3 + 4 + 5 + 6) + (7 + 8 + 9 + 10 + \ldots + 44)$.

So $(7 + 8 + 9 + 10 + \ldots + 50) - (1 + 2 + 3 + 4 + \ldots + 44) =$

$(45 + 46 + 47 + 48 + 49 + 50) - (1 + 2 + 3 + 4 + 5 + 6) =$

$(45 - 1) + (46 - 2) + (47 - 3) + (48 - 4) + (49 - 5) + (50 - 6) =$

$44 + 44 + 44 + 44 + 44 + 44 = 6(44) = 264$.

USING THE CALCULATOR TO SAVE TIME

Of course, there will be many questions for which using a calculator can save you time. Here's an ACT trig question that's much easier with a calculator:

2. $\sin 495° =$

F. $-\dfrac{\sqrt{2}}{2}$

G. $-\dfrac{1}{2}$

H. $\dfrac{1}{2}$

J. $\dfrac{\sqrt{2}}{2}$

K. $\dfrac{3\sqrt{2}}{2}$

Without a calculator, this is a very difficult problem. To find a trigonometric function of an angle greater than or equal to 90°, sketch a circle of radius 1 and centered at the origin of the coordinate grid. Start from the point (1, 0) and rotate the appropriate number of degrees counterclockwise. When you rotate counterclockwise 495°, you rotate 360° (which brings you back to where you started), and then an additional 135°. That puts you 45° into the second quadrant. Now you need to know whether sine is positive or negative in the second quadrant. Pretty scary, huh?

With a calculator, this problem becomes simple. Just punch in "sin 495°" and you get 0.7071067811865. (F) and (G) are negative, so they're out, and 0.7071067811865 is clearly not equal to $\dfrac{1}{2}$, so (H) is also wrong. That leaves only (J) or (K). Now, $\dfrac{3\sqrt{2}}{2}$ is

greater than 1, so if you multiply it by another number greater than

1 (namely $\frac{3}{2}$), the result is obviously greater than 1. So you can eliminate (K), leaving (J) as the correct answer. With a calculator, you can get this question right without really understanding it.

CALCULATORS: THE GAME PLAN

The key to effective calculator use is practice, so don't buy one the night before the test. If you don't already have a calculator (and intend to use one on the test), buy one now. Make sure you buy an extra set of fresh batteries that you can bring with you on test day. You don't want to be stuck with a dead calculator in the middle of a question! Unless you plan to study math or science in college, you won't need anything more complex than trig functions. Bear in mind that you're better off bringing a simple model that you're familiar with than an esoteric model you don't know how to use.

The following calculators are allowed on the test: pocket organizers, computers, models with writing pads, computers with QWERTY keyboards, paper tapes, power cords, wireless transmitters, noisy calculators, Kray supercomputers.

Know Your Calculator

Practicing with your calculator is the best way to get a sense of where it can help and save time.

3. $(7.3 + 0.8) - 3(1.98 + 0.69) =$

   A. –0.99

   B. –0.09

   C. 0

   D. 0.09

   E. 0.99

This problem basically involves straightforward computation, so you'd be right if you reached for your calculator. However, if you just start punching the numbers in as they appear in the question, you might come up with the wrong answer. When you're performing a string of computations you know that you need to follow the right order of operations. The problem is, your calculator might not know this. Some calculators have parentheses keys and do follow PEMDAS, so it's important to know your machine and what its capabilities are. PEMDAS stands for *Parentheses* first, then *Exponents*, then *Multiplication and Division* (left to right), and last, *Addition and Subtraction* (left to right).

If your calculator doesn't follow the order of operations, you'd need to perform the operations within parentheses separately. You'd get $8.1 - 3(2.67)$. Multiplication comes before subtraction, so you'd get $8.1 - 8.01$, and then finally .09, choice D.

4. A certain bank issues 3-letter identification codes to its customers. If each letter can be used only once per code, how many different codes are possible?

    F.   26

    G.   78

    H.   326

    J. 15,600

    K. 17,576

For the first letter in the code you can choose any of the 26 letters in the alphabet. For the second letter, you can choose from all the letters except the one you used in the first spot, so there are $26 - 1 = 25$ possibilities. For the third there are $26 - 2 = 24$ possibilities. So the total number of different codes possible is equal to $26 \times 25 \times 24$. Using your calculator you find there are 15,600 codes—choice J.

Backsolve

A calculator can help you in backsolving (plugging the answer choices back into the question stem) and picking numbers (substituting numbers for the variables in the question).

5. Which of the following fractions is greater than 0.68 and less than 0.72 ?

    A. $\frac{5}{9}$

    B. $\frac{3}{5}$

    C. $\frac{7}{11}$

    D. $\frac{2}{3}$

    E. $\frac{5}{7}$

Here you have to convert the fractions in the answer choices to decimals and see which one falls in the range of values given to you in the question. If you're familiar with common decimal and fraction conversions, you might know that choice B, $\frac{3}{5}$ = .6, is too small and choice D, $\frac{2}{3}$, approximately .67, is also too small. But you'd still have to check out the other three choices. Your calculator can make short work of this, showing you that choice A, $\frac{5}{9}$ = .$\overline{55}$, choice C, $\frac{7}{11}$ = .$\overline{63}$, and choice E, $\frac{5}{7}$, is approximately .71. Only 0.71 falls between 0.68 and 0.72, so E is correct.

STEP 8: ALGEBRA, PERCENTS, AND AVERAGES

The main idea of the first Math step was: Don't jump in head first and start crunching numbers until you've given the problem some thought. Make sure you know what you're doing, *and* that what you're doing won't take too long.

As we saw, sometimes you'll know how to proceed as soon as you understand the question. A good number of ACT algebra and coordinate geometry questions are straightforward textbook questions you may already be prepared for.

TEXTBOOK ALGEBRA AND COORDINATE GEOMETRY

When you take the ACT, you can be sure you'll see some of the following questions with only slight variations. We're assuming that you know how to do these basic kinds of questions. If not, you probably want to pick up Kaplan's larger ACT book, which contains an appendix covering these basic techniques. You might also consider putting off your test, if possible. If you don't know how to multiply binomials, factor a polynomial, or solve a quadratic equation by now, you probably won't be ready to take the test in just a few weeks.

By test day, then, you should know how to do the following:

Part Three: The ACT Math Test

1. Evaluate an algebraic expression.
   Example: If $x = -2$, then $x^2 + 5x - 6 = $?

2. Multiply binomials.
   Example: $(x + 3)(x + 4) = $?

3. Factor a polynomial.
   Example: What is the complete factorization of $x^2 - 5x + 6$?

4. Solve a quadratic equation.
   Example: If $x^2 + 12 = 7x$, what are the two possible values of x ?

5. Simplify an algebraic fraction.
   Example: For all $x \neq \pm 3$, $\dfrac{x^2 - x - 12}{x^2 - 9} = $?

6. Solve a linear equation.
   Example: If $5x - 12 = -2x + 9$, then $x = $?

7. Solve a system of equations.
   Example: If $4x + 3y = 8$, and $x + y = 3$, what is the value of x ?

8. Solve an inequality.
   Example: What are all the values of x for which $-5x + 7 < -3$?

9. Find the distance between two points in the (x, y) coordinate plane.
   Example: What is the distance between the points with (x, y) coordinates $(-2, 2)$ and $(1, -2)$?

10. Find the slope of a line from its equation.
    Example: What is the slope of the line with the equation $2x + 3y = 4$?

KAPLAN

These questions are all so straightforward and traditional, they could have come out of a high school algebra textbook. These are the questions you should do the way you were taught.

IF YOU DON'T KNOW YOUR BASIC ALGEBRA AND COORDINATE GEOMETRY, CONSIDER POSTPONING THE TEST AND USING THE MATH APPENDIX IN KAPLAN'S FULL-LENGTH ACT BOOK.

NONTEXTBOOK ALGEBRA AND COORDINATE GEOMETRY

The techniques you'd use on textbook questions are the techniques you've been taught in high school math classes. We're not so concerned in this book with such problems. Here we're focused on algebra and coordinate geometry situations where the quick and reliable solution method is not so obvious, and where often the best method is one your algebra teacher never taught you.

It's bound to happen at some point during the test. You look at a math problem and you don't see what to do. Don't freak out. Think about the problem for a few seconds before you give up. When you don't see the quick and reliable approach right away, shake up the problem a little. Try one of these "shake-it-up" techniques:

1. Restate the problem.
2. Remove the disguise.
3. Pick numbers.
4. Backsolve.

1. RESTATE THE PROBLEM

Often the way to get over that stymied feeling is to change your perspective. Have you ever watched people playing Scrabble™? In their search to form high-scoring words from their seven letters, they continually move the tiles around in their racks. Sometimes a good word becomes apparent only after rearranging the tiles. One might not see the seven-letter word in this arrangement:

R E B A G L A

But just reverse the tiles and a word almost reveals itself:

A L G A B E R

The same gimmick works on the ACT, too. When you get stuck, try looking at the problem from a different angle. Rearrange the numbers or change fractions to decimals. Or, factor, or multiply out, or redraw the diagram. Do anything that might give you a fresh perspective.

Here's a question you might not know how to handle at first glance:

1. Which of the following is equivalent to $7^{77} - 7^{76}$?

    A. 7
    B. 7^{77-76}
    C. $7^{77 \div 76}$
    D. $7(77-76)$
    E. $7^{76}(6)$

Here's a hint: Think of an easier problem testing the same principles. The important thing to look for is the basic relationships involved—here, we have exponents and subtraction. That subtraction sign causes trouble, because none of the ordinary rules of exponents seem to apply when there is subtraction of "unlike" terms.

Another hint: How would you work with $x^2 - x$? Most test takers could come up with another expression for $x^2 - x$: They'd factor to $x(x - 1)$. So if the problem asked for $x^{77} - x^{76}$, they'd factor to

$x^{76}(x-1)$. The rule is no different for 7 than for x. Factoring out the 7^{76} gives you: $7^{76}(7-1)$, which is $7^{76}(6)$, or choice (E).

ON A COMPLEX QUESTION, THINK OF HOW YOU WOULD HANDLE AN EASY PROBLEM THAT TESTS THE SAME PRINCIPLE.

Sometimes an algebra question will include an expression that isn't of much use in its given form. Try restating the expression by either simplifying it or factoring it. For example:

2. If $\frac{x}{2} - \frac{x}{6}$ is an integer, which of the following statements must be true?

    F. x is positive.

    G. x is odd.

    H. x is even.

    J. x is a multiple of 3.

    K. x is a multiple of 6.

Reexpress it as: $\dfrac{x}{2} - \dfrac{x}{6} = \dfrac{3x}{6} - \dfrac{x}{6} = \dfrac{2x}{6} = \dfrac{x}{3}$

This form of the expression tells us a lot more. If $\frac{x}{3}$ is an integer, then x is equal to 3 times an integer:

$$\frac{x}{3} = \text{an integer}$$

$$x = 3 \times (\text{an integer})$$

In other words, x is a multiple of 3, choice J.

RESTATE EXPRESSIONS THAT DON'T MAKE IMMEDIATE SENSE.

2. REMOVE THE DISGUISE

Sometimes it's hard to see the quick and reliable method right away because the true nature of the problem is hidden behind a disguise. Look at this example:

3. What are the (x, y) coordinates of the point of intersection of the line representing the equation $5x + 2y = 4$ and the line representing the equation $x - 2y = 8$?

    A. (2, 3)

    B. (−2, 3)

    C. (2, −3)

    D. (−3, 2)

    E. (3, −2)

This may look like a coordinate geometry question, but do you really have to graph the lines to find the point of intersection? Remember, the ACT is looking for creative thinkers, not mindless calculators! Think about it—what's the significance of the point of intersection, the one point that the two lines have in common? That's the one point whose coordinates will satisfy both equations.

So what we realize now is that this is not a coordinate geometry question at all, but a "system of equations" question. All it's really asking you to do is solve the pair of equations for x and y. The question has nothing to do with slopes, intercepts, axes, or quadrants. It's a pure algebra question in disguise.

Now that we know we're looking at a system of equations, the method of solution presents itself more clearly. The first equation has $x + 2y$, and the second equation has $x − 2y$. If we just "add" the equations, the y terms cancel:

$$5x + 2y = 4$$
$$\underline{x - 2y = 8}$$
$$6x\ \ \ = 12$$

If $6x = 12$, then $x = 2$. Plug that back into either of the original equations and you'll find that $y = -3$. The point of intersection is $(2, -3)$, and the answer is C.

4. A geometer uses the following formula to estimate the area A of the shaded portion of a circle as shown in the figure below when only the height h and the length of the chord c are known:

$$A = \frac{2ch}{3} + \frac{h^3}{2c}$$

What is the geometer's estimate of the area, in square inches, of the shaded region if the height is 2 inches and the length of the chord is 6 inches?

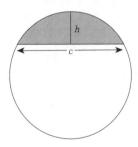

F. 6

G. $6\frac{2}{3}$

H. $7\frac{1}{2}$

J. $8\frac{2}{3}$

K. 12

At first glance this looks like a horrendously esoteric geometry question. Who ever heard of such a formula?

But when you think about the question, you realize that you don't really have to understand the formula. In fact, this is not a geometry question at all; it's really just an "evaluate the algebraic expression" question in disguise. All you have to do is plug the given values $h = 2$ and $c = 6$ into the given formula:

$$A = \frac{2ch}{3} + \frac{h^3}{2c}$$

$$= \frac{2(6)(2)}{3} + \frac{2^3}{2(6)}$$

$$= 8 + \frac{2}{3} = 8\frac{2}{3}$$

Choice J is correct.

The people who wrote this question wanted you to freak out at first sight and give up. Don't give up on a question too quickly just because it looks like it's testing something you never saw before. In many such cases it's really a familiar problem in disguise.

> **A COMPLEX PROBLEM IS OFTEN JUST AN EASIER PROBLEM IN DISGUISE.**

3. PICK NUMBERS

Sometimes you can get stuck on an algebra problem just because it's too general or abstract. A good way to get a handle on such a problem is to make it more explicit by temporarily substituting particular numbers for the variables. For example:

5. If *a* is an odd integer and *b* is an even integer, which of the following must be odd?

    A. $2a + b$

    B. $a + 2b$

    C. ab

    D. a^2b

    E. ab^2

Rather than try to think this one through abstractly, it's easier to pick numbers for *a* and *b*. There are rules that predict the evenness or oddness of sums, differences, and products, but there's no need to memorize those rules. When it comes to adding, subtracting, and multiplying evens and odds, what happens with one pair of numbers generally happens with all similar pairs.

Just say, for the time being, that $a = 1$ and $b = 2$. Plug those values into the answer choices, and there's a good chance only one choice will be odd:

    A. $2a + b = 2(1) + 2 = 4$

    B. $a + 2b = 1 + 2(2) = 5$

    C. $ab = (1)(2) = 2$

    D. $a^2b = (1)^2(2) = 2$

    E. $ab^2 = (1)(2)^2 = 4$

Choice B was the only odd one for $a = 1$ and $b = 2$, so it *must* be the one that's odd no matter *what* odd number *a* is and even number *b* is.

MAKE ABSTRACT PROBLEMS CONCRETE BY SUBSTITUTING NUMBERS FOR VARIABLES.

4. BACKSOLVE

With some math problems, it may actually be easier to try out each answer choice until you find the one that works, rather than try to solve the problem and then look among the choices for the answer. Since this approach involves working backwards from the answer choices to the question stem, it's called backsolving. Here's a good example:

6. All 200 tickets were sold for a particular concert. Some tickets cost $10 apiece, and the others cost $5 apiece. If total ticket sales were $1,750, how many of the more expensive tickets were sold?

    F. 20

    G. 75

    H. 100

    J. 150

    K. 175

There are ways to solve this problem by setting up an equation or two, but if you're not comfortable with the algebraic approach to this one, why not just try out each answer choice?

The answer choices are generally listed in numerical order, and if the first number you try doesn't work, the process of plugging in that first number might tell you whether you'll need a smaller or a larger number. So when backsolving, start off with the middle choice (choice C or H) to be safe.

So, start with choice H. If 100 tickets went for $10, then the other 100 went for $5. The cost of 100 tickets at $10 is $1,000, and 100 tickets at $5 is $500, for a total of $1,500—too small. There must have been more than 100 $10 tickets.

Try choice J next. If 150 tickets went for $10, then the other 50 went for $5. The cost of 150 tickets at $10 is $1,500, and 50 tickets at $5 is $250, for a total of $1,750—that's it! The answer is J.

Backsolving your way to the answer may not be a method you'd show your algebra teacher with pride, but your algebra teacher won't be watching while you take the test. Remember, all that matters is right answers—it doesn't matter how you get them.

> **WHEN BACKSOLVING, START WITH THE MIDDLE CHOICE, C (OR H).**

STORY PROBLEMS

We find that about one-third of the questions on the Math subtest are story problems. Although some story problems present unique situations that must be analyzed on the spot, others are just variations on familiar themes.

PERCENT PROBLEMS

In percent problems, you're usually given two numbers and asked to find a third. The key is to identify what you have and what you're looking for.

> **IN PERCENT PROBLEMS, IDENTIFY THE PART, THE PERCENT, AND THE WHOLE, AND REMEMBER THAT PART = PERCENT × WHOLE.**

Put the numbers and the unknown into the general form:

(Usually the part is associated with the word *is* and the whole is associated with the word *of*.)

For example:

7. In a group of 250 students, 40 are seniors. What percentage of the group is seniors?

   A. 1.6 percent

   B. 6.25 percent

   C. 10 percent

   D. 16 percent

   E. 40 percent

The percent is what we're looking for ("What percentage . . ."); the whole is 250 (". . . of the group . . ."); and the part is 40 (". . . is seniors"). Plug these into the general formula:

$$\text{Part} = \text{Percent} \times \text{Whole}$$
$$40 = 250x$$
$$x = \frac{40}{250} = .16 = 16 \text{ percent, choice D}$$

Percent Increase/Decrease Problems

Many ACT percent problems concern percent change. To increase a number by a certain percent, calculate that percent of the original number and add it on. To decrease a number by a certain percent, calculate that percent of the original number and subtract. For example, to answer "What number is 30 percent greater than 80?" find 30 percent of 80—that's 24—and add that onto 80: 80 + 24 = 104.

The ACT has ways of complicating percent change problems. Especially tricky are problems with multiple changes, such as a percent increase followed by another percent increase, or a percent increase followed by a percent decrease.

Here's a question, for example, that's not as simple as it seems:

8. If a positive number is increased by 70 percent, and then the result is decreased by 50 percent, which of the following accurately describes the net change?

   F. a 20 percent decrease

   G. a 15 percent decrease

   H. a 12 percent increase

   J. a 20 percent increase

   K. a 120 percent increase

The way to get a handle on this one is to pick a number. Suppose the original number is 100. After a 70 percent increase it rises to 170. That number, 170, is decreased by 50 percent, which means it's reduced by half to 85. The net change from 100 to 85 is a 15 percent decrease—choice G.

DON'T JUST ADD AND SUBTRACT PERCENTS. PICK 100 AS THE ORIGINAL NUMBER AND WORK FROM THERE.

AVERAGE PROBLEMS

Instead of giving you a list of values to plug into the average formula, ACT average questions often have a slight spin. They tell you the average of a group of terms and ask you to find the value of the missing term. Here's a classic example:

9. To earn a B for the semester, Linda needs an average of at least 80 on the five tests. Her average for the first four test scores is 79. What is the minimum score she must get on the fifth test to earn a B for the semester?

   A. 80

   B. 81

   C. 82

   D. 83

   E. 84

The key to almost every average question is to use the sum. Sums can be combined much more readily than averages. An average of 80 on five tests is more usefully thought of as a combined score of 400. To get a B for the semester, Linda's five test scores have to add up to 400 or more. The first four scores add up to $4 \times 79 = 316$. She needs another 84 to get that 316 up to 400 The answer is E.

Weighted Average Problems

Another spin ACT test makers use is to give you an average for part of a group and an average for the rest of the group and then ask for the combined average.

> **TO GET A COMBINED AVERAGE, IT'S USUALLY WRONG JUST TO AVERAGE THE AVERAGES.**

For example:

10. In a class of 10 boys and 15 girls, the boys' average score on the final exam was 80 and the girls' average score was 90. What was the average score for the whole class?

    F. 83

    G. 84

    H. 85

    J. 86

    K. 87

Don't just average 80 and 90 to get 85. That would work only if the class had exactly the same number of girls as boys. In this case, there are more girls, so they carry more "weight" in the overall class average. In other words, the class average should be somewhat closer to 90 (the girls' average) than to 80 (the boys' average).

As usual with averages, the key is to use the sum. The average score for the whole class is the total of the 25 individual scores divided by 25. We don't have 25 scores to add up, but we can use the boys' average and the girls' average to get two subtotals.

If 10 boys average 80, then their ten scores add up to 10×80, or 800 total. If 15 girls average 90, then their 15 scores add up to 15×90, or 1,350 total. Add the boys' total to the girls' total: $800 + 1,350 = 2,150$. That's the class total, which can be divided by 25 to get the class average: $\frac{2,150}{25} = 86$. The answer is J.

PROBABILITY PROBLEMS

Probabilities are part-to-whole ratios. The whole is the total number of possible outcomes. The part is the number of "favorable" outcomes. For example, if a drawer contains two black ties and five other ties, and you want a black tie, the total number of possible outcomes is 7 (the total number of ties) and the number of "favorable" outcomes is 2 (the number of black ties). The probability of choosing a black tie at random is $\frac{2}{7}$.

> **REMEMBER, THE PROBABILITY OF WHAT WILL HAPPEN IS NOT AFFECTED BY WHAT HAS HAPPENED ALREADY.**

Because more than half the math questions on the ACT involve algebra, it's a good idea to take some time before the day of the test to solidify your understanding of the basics. Keep things in perspective. Geometry's important, too, but algebra's more important.

STEP 9:
GEOMETRY

The ACT Math test typically has 14 geometry questions and 4 trigonometry questions. Depending on what kind of score you're aiming for, you might be able to blow off those few trigonometry questions. But you probably don't want to blow off many geometry questions.

Fortunately, a good number of the geometry questions are straightforward. Nothing is distorted or disguised. With these questions you know what to do—if you know your geometry—the instant you understand them.

TEXTBOOK GEOMETRY QUESTIONS

When you take the ACT you'll see a few questions requiring you to do some of the actions cited below. These are straightforward geometry tasks, and if you don't know how to do them by now, we recommend that you not take the ACT until you do. Again we refer you to the math appendix in Kaplan's more comprehensive prep book, *ACT*.

- **Finding the area of a square or other rectangle**
  The formula for the area of a rectangle is $A = l \times w$.
- **Finding the area of a circle**
  The formula for the area of a circle is $A = \pi r^2$, where r is the radius.
- **Finding the area of a trapezoid**
  The formula for the area of a trapezoid is

  $A = \left(\dfrac{b_1 + b_2}{2} \right) h$, where b_1 and b_2 are the lengths of the

  parallel sides.
- **Working with isosceles and equilateral triangles**
- **Working with special right triangles**
  45–45–90; 30–60–90; etcetera
- **Using the Pythagorean theorem**
  The Pythagorean theorem says:
  $(\text{leg}_1)^2 + (\text{leg}_2)^2 = (\text{hypotenuse})^2$, or $a^2 + b^2 = c^2$.
- **Working with similar triangles**
- **Working with parallel lines and transversals**
- **Finding the area of a triangle**
  The formula for the area of a triangle is $A = \dfrac{1}{2}bh$.
- **Figuring the length of an arc**

IF YOU DON'T KNOW YOUR BASIC GEOMETRY, CONSIDER
POSTPONING YOUR ACT.

NONTEXTBOOK GEOMETRY QUESTIONS

As if it weren't hard enough to remember all the facts and formulas
needed for problems like the questions above, the test makers have
ways of further complicating geometry questions.

HIDDEN INFORMATION

Some ACT geometry questions are not all that they seem. It's not always obvious what the question's getting at. Sometimes you really have to think about the figure and the given information before that light bulb goes off in your head. Often the inspiration that brings illumination is finding the hidden information.

Here's an example that doesn't come right out and say what it's all about:

1. In the figure below, $\triangle ABC$ is a right triangle and $\overline{AC}$ is perpendicular to $\overline{BD}$. If $\overline{AB}$ is 6 units long, and $\overline{AC}$ is 10 units long, how many units long is $\overline{AD}$?

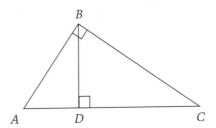

A. 3

B. $2\sqrt{3}$

C. 3.6

D. 4

E. $3\sqrt{2}$

At first this looks like a Pythagorean theorem question. In fact, the two given sides of $\triangle ABC$ identify it as the 6-8-10 version of the 3-4-5 special right triangle. So we know that $BC = 8$. So what? What good does that do us? How's that going to help us find AD?

The inspiration here is to realize that this is a "similar triangles" problem. We don't see the word *similar* anywhere in the question stem, but the stem and the figure combined actually tell us that all three triangles in the figure—$\triangle ABC$, $\triangle ADB$, and $\triangle BDC$—are similar. We know the triangles are similar because they all have the same three angles. Here are the three triangles separated and oriented to show the correspondences:

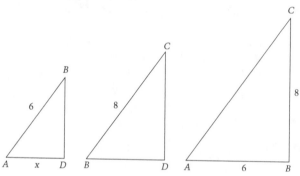

In this orientation it's easy to see the proportion setup that will solve the problem:

$$\frac{10}{6} = \frac{6}{x}$$

$$10x = 36$$

$$x = 3.6, \text{ choice C}$$

IF YOU FIND YOURSELF STUCK ON A PROBLEM, LOOK FOR HIDDEN INFORMATION.

Here's another example with hidden information:

2. In the figure below, the area of the circle centered at O is 25π, and $\overline{AC}$ is perpendicular to $\overline{OB}$. If $\overline{AC}$ is 8 units long, how many units long is $\overline{BD}$?

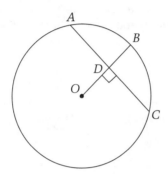

F. 2

G. 2.5

H. 3

J. 3.125

K. 4

This is a tough one. It's not easy to see how to get BD from the given information. We can use the area—25π—to figure out the radius, and then we'd know the length of OB :

$$\text{Area} = \pi r^2$$
$$25\pi = \pi r^2$$
$$25 = r^2$$
$$r = 5$$

So we know $OB = 5$, but what about BD? If we knew OD, we could subtract that from OB to get what we want. But do we know OD? This is where most people get stuck.

The inspiration that will lead to a solution is that we can take advantage of the right angle at D. Look what happens when we take a pencil and physically add $\overline{OA}$ and $\overline{OC}$ to the figure:

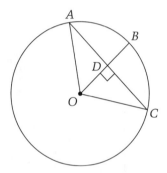

$\triangle OAD$ and $\triangle OCD$ are right triangles. And when we write in the lengths, we discover some special right triangles:

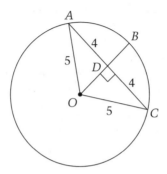

Now it's apparent that $OD = 3$. Since $OB = 5$, BD is $5 - 3 = 2$. The answer is F.

DON'T BE AFRAID TO PENCIL IN ADDITIONS TO THE GIVEN DIAGRAMS.

FIGURELESS PROBLEMS

Some ACT geometry problems present an extra challenge because they don't provide a figure. You have to "figure it out" for yourself. Try this one:

3. If one side of a right triangle is 3 units long, and a second side is 4 units long, which of the following could be the length, in units, of the third side?

   A. 1

   B. 2

   C. $\sqrt{7}$

   D. $3\sqrt{2}$

   E. $3\sqrt{3}$

The key to solving most figureless problems is to sketch a diagram, but sometimes that's not so easy because you're given less information than you might like. Question 3 is the perfect example. It gives you two sides of a right triangle and asks for the third. Sounds familiar. And the two sides it gives you—3 and 4—really sound familiar. It's a 3-4-5, right?

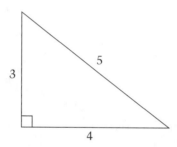

So the answer's 5 . . . whoops! There's no 5 among the answer choices! What's going on?

Better check back. Notice that the question asks, "which of the following could be the length . . . ?" That *could* is crucial. It suggests that there's more than one possibility. Our answer of 5 was too obvious. There's another one somewhere.

Can you think of another way of sketching the figure with the same given information? Who says that the 3 and 4 have to be the two legs? Look at what happens when you make one of them—the larger one, of course—the *hypotenuse*:

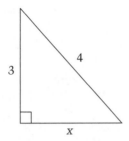

This is not a 3-4-5 triangle, because in a 3-4-5 the 3 and the 4 are the legs. This is not a special right triangle. To figure out the length of the third side, we'll just have to resort to the Pythagorean theorem:

$$(\text{leg}_1)^2 + (\text{leg}_2)^2 = (\text{hypotenuse})^2$$

$$3^2 + x^2 = 4^2$$
$$9 + x^2 = 16$$
$$x^2 = 7$$
$$x = \sqrt{7}$$

The answer is C.

SKETCH YOUR OWN FIGURES FOR FIGURELESS PROBLEMS.

MULTI-STEP PROBLEMS

Some of the toughest ACT geometry questions take many steps to solve and combine different geometry concepts. Here's an example:

4. In the figure below, $\overline{AB}$ is tangent to the circle at _A_. If the circumference of the circle is 12π units and $\overline{OB}$ is 12 units long, what is the area, in square units, of the shaded region?

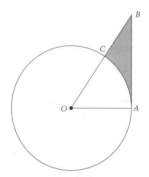

F. $18\sqrt{3} - 6\pi$

G. $24\sqrt{3} - 6\pi$

H. $18\sqrt{3} - 2\pi$

J. $12\pi - 12$

K. $24\sqrt{3} - 2\pi$

This is about as hard as they come on the ACT. It's by no means clear how the given information—the circumference of the circle and the length of $\overline{OB}$ —will lead us to the area of the shaded region.

So what do you do? Give up? No.

Don't give up immediately unless you're really short on time or you know for sure you can't do the problem. So then should you just plow ahead blindly and figure out every length, angle, and area you can and see where that leads?

Well, *not exactly*. It would be better to be more systematic.

The key to success with a circuitous problem like this is to focus on your destination—what you're looking for—and think about what you need to get there.

Our destination in question 4 is "the area of the shaded region." That region is a shape that has no name, let alone an area formula. Like most shaded regions, this one is the difference between two familiar shapes with names and area formulas. Think of the shaded region in question 4 as:

(the area of ∆*AOB*) − (the area of sector *AOC*)

So, we now know that we need to figure out the area of the triangle and the area of the sector.

First, the triangle. We are explicitly given $OB = 12$. We are also given that $\overline{AB}$ is tangent to the circle at A, which tells us that $\overline{OA}$ is a radius and that $\angle OAB$ is a right angle. So if we can figure out the radius of the circle, we'll have two sides of a right triangle, which will enable us to figure out the third side, and then figure out the area.

We can get the radius from the given circumference. Plug what we know into the formula and solve for r:

$$\text{Circumference} = 2\pi r$$
$$12\pi = 2\pi r$$
$$r = \frac{12\pi}{2\pi} = 6$$

$\overline{OA} = 6$. Aha! So it turns out that ∆*AOB* is no ordinary right triangle. Since one leg—6—is exactly half the hypotenuse—12—we're looking at a 30-60-90 triangle. By applying the well-known side ratios ($1:\sqrt{3}:2$) for a 30-60-90 triangle, we determine that $\overline{AB} = 6\sqrt{3}$.

Now we can plug the lengths of the legs in for the base and altitude in the formula for the area of a triangle:

$$\text{Area} = \frac{1}{2}bh$$

$$= \frac{1}{2}(6\sqrt{3})(6)$$

$$= 18\sqrt{3}$$

Already it looks like the answer's going to be F or H—they're the choices that begin with $18\sqrt{3}$. We could just guess F or H and move on, but if we've come this far, we might as well go all the way.

Next, the area of the sector. Fortunately, while working on the triangle, we figured out the two things we need to get the area of the sector: the radius of the circle (6) and the measure of the central angle (60°). The radius tells us that the area of the whole circle (πr^2) is 36π. And the central angle tells us that the area of the sector is $\frac{60}{360}$ or $\frac{1}{6}$ of the area of the circle. $\frac{1}{6}$ of 36π is 6π. So the area of the shaded region is $18\sqrt{3} - 6\pi$, choice F.

BREAK DOWN COMPLEX PROBLEMS INTO SIMPLER STEPS.

A final bit of advice: Your goal on the ACT is to get as many points as possible, so focus your studies on the areas that are likely to generate the most points. Together, algebra and plane geometry make up the vast majority of ACT Math questions, so make sure you know how to do the basics in these areas.

THE ACT READING TEST

Step 10:
The Key to ACT Reading

The kind of reading rewarded by the ACT may not be what you expect. You may think that success on a test like this requires that you read very slowly and deliberately, making sure you remember everything. Well, we at Kaplan have found that this kind of reading won't work on the ACT. In fact, it's a sure way to run out of time halfway through the Reading test.

The real key to ACT reading is to read very quickly but actively, getting a sense of the gist, or "main idea," of the passage and seeing how everything fits together to support that main idea. You should constantly try to think ahead. Look for the general outline of the passage—how it's structured. Don't worry about the details. You'll come back for those later.

READ ACTIVELY, WITH AN EYE TOWARD WHERE THE AUTHOR IS GOING.

Fast, active reading, of course, requires a little more mental energy than slow, passive reading. But it pays off. Those who dwell on details—who passively let the passage reveal itself at its own pace—are sure to run out of time. Don't be that kind of reader! Again, the key is *take control.* Make the passage reveal itself to you on *your* schedule by skimming the passage, with an eye on structure rather than detail. Look for keywords that tell you what the author is doing, so that you can save yourself time. For example, read examples very, very quickly, just glancing over the words. When an author says "for example," you know that what follows is an example of a general point. Do you need to understand that specific example? Maybe, maybe not. If you *do*, you can come back and read the verbiage when you're attacking the questions. You'll know exactly where the author gave an example of general point *x* (or whatever). If you *don't* need to know the example for any of the questions, great! You haven't wasted much time on something that won't get you a point.

STRUCTURAL CLUES

To help you know where an author is going, pay careful attention to "structural clues" (we discussed these briefly in English I). Words such as *but*, *nevertheless*, and *moreover* help you get a sense of where a piece of writing is going. You also should look for signal phrases such as *clearly, as a result,* or *no one can deny that* to determine the logic of the passage. Remember, you can come back for the details later, when you're doing the questions. What's important in reading the passage is to get a sense of how those details fit together to express the point or points of the passage.

For your reference, we've gathered together some important ways in which an author "tells" you where a reading passage is going.

COMMON STRUCTURAL CLUES

Indicating a contrast

   but

   however

   on the other hand

   nevertheless

Indicating a continuation with a similar or complementary thought

   moreover

   furthermore

   ; (a semicolon)

Indicating a conclusion

   therefore

   thus

Indicating reasons for a conclusion

   since

   because of

   due to

Indicating an example or illustration

   for instance

   for example

Now let's see how you can use this skill of active reading to develop a plan of attack for the ACT Reading section.

KAPLAN'S THREE-STEP METHOD

You must always remember that when reading for the ACT, you have a special purpose: to answer specific multiple-choice questions. And we've found that the best way to do this is initially to read a passage quickly and actively for general understanding, then refer to the passage to answer individual questions. Not everybody should use the exact same strategy, but we find that almost every ACT test taker can succeed by following these three basic steps:

- Preread the passage quickly.
- Consider the question stem.
- Refer to the passage (before looking at the choices).

For most students, these three tasks should together take up about nine minutes per passage. Less than three of those nine minutes should be spent prereading. The remaining time should be devoted to considering the questions and referring to the passage to check your answers. As we mentioned earlier, you probably want to take two sweeps through the questions for each passage, getting the doable ones the first time around, and coming back for the harder ones.

STEP 1: Preread the Passage

Prereading means quickly working through the passage before trying to answer the questions. Remember to "know where you're going," using structural clues to anticipate how the parts of the passage fit together. In this prereading, the main goals are:

- To understand the gist of the passage (the "main idea").
- To get an overall idea of how the passage is organized—a kind of road map—so that it will be easier to refer to later.

You may want to underline key points, jot down notes, circle structural clues—whatever it takes to accomplish the two goals above. You may even want to label each paragraph, to fix in your mind how the paragraphs relate to one another and what aspect of the main idea is discussed in each. That could be your road map.

An important reminder: *Don't read slowly, and don't get bogged down in individual details.* Most of the details in the passage aren't required for answering the questions, so why waste time worrying about them?

DON'T GET BOGGED DOWN IN THE DETAILS OF THE PASSAGE.

STEP 2: Consider the Question Stem

Approaching the reading questions requires self-discipline. Most test takers have an almost irresistible urge to immediately jump to the answer choices to see what "looks OK." That's not a good idea. Don't let the answer choices direct your thinking. The test makers intentionally design the answers to confuse you if they can.

DON'T LET THE ANSWER CHOICES DIRECT YOUR THINKING.

In Reading, you should think about the question stem (the part above the answer choices) *without looking at the choices.* In most questions, you won't be able to remember exactly what the passage said about the matter in question. That's all right. In fact, even if you do think you remember, don't trust your memory. Instead . . .

STEP 3: Refer to the Passage

You won't be rereading the whole passage, of course. But look for the place where the answer to a question can be found (the question stem will sometimes contain a line reference to help you out; otherwise, rely on your road map of the passage). Your chosen answer should match the passage—not in exact vocabulary, perhaps, but in meaning.

> **ALWAYS REFER TO THE PASSAGE BEFORE CHOOSING AN ANSWER.**

PRACTICING PREREADING

Now practice prereading on the full-length ACT passage that follows. We're not going to give you the questions until Step 11, when we'll talk about the different kinds of Reading questions and how to answer them. For now, just worry about the prereading part of the Kaplan three-step method. Take three minutes or so, and preread the passage. Remember to read quickly, with an eye to the structure of the passage. Make yourself a road map for the passage. And—most important of all—keep track of time and don't get bogged down in details!

Tragedy was the invention of the Greeks. In their Golden Age, the fifth century before Christ, they produced the world's greatest dramatists, new forms of tragedy and comedy that have been models ever
5 since, and a theatre that every age goes back to for rediscovery of some basic principles. . . .

Since it derived from primitive religious rites, with masks and ceremonial costumes, and made use of music, dance, and poetry, the Greek drama
10 was at the opposite pole from the modern realistic stage. In fact, probably no other theatre in history has made fuller use of the intensities of art. The masks, made of painted linen, wood, and plaster, brought down from primitive days the atmosphere
15 of gods, heroes, and demons. Our nineteenth-and twentieth-century grandfathers thought masks must have been very artificial. Today, however, we appreciate their exciting intensity and can see that in a large theatre they were indispensable. If they
20 allowed no fleeting change of expression during a single episode, they could give for each episode in turn more intense expression than any human face could. When Oedipus comes back with bleeding eyes, the new mask could be more terrible than any
25 facial makeup the audience could endure, yet in its sculpted intensity more beautiful than a real face.

Most essential of all intensities, and hardest for us to understand, was the chorus. Yet many play wrights today are trying to find some equivalent to
30 do for a modern play what the chorus did for the Greeks. During the episodes played by the actors, the chorus would only provide a background of group response, enlarging and reverberating the

35 emotions of the actors, sometimes protesting and opposing but in general serving as ideal spectators to stir and lead the reactions of the audience. But between episodes, with the actors out of the way, the chorus took over. We have only the words, not the music or dance, and some translations of the

40 odes are in such formal, old-fashioned language that it is hard to guess that they were accompanied by vigorous, sometimes even wild dances and symbolic actions that filled an orchestra that in some cities was sixty to ninety feet in diameter.

45 Sometimes the chorus expressed simple horror or lament. Sometimes it chanted and acted out, in unison and in precise formations of rows and lines, the acts of violence the characters were enacting offstage. When Phaedra rushes offstage in

50 *Hippolytus* to hang herself from the rafters, the members of the chorus, all fifteen of them, perform in mime and chant the act of tying the rope and swinging from the rafters. Sometimes the chorus tells or reenacts an incident of history or legend

55 that throws light on the situation in the play. Sometimes the chorus puts into specific action what is a general intention in the mind of the main character. When Oedipus resolves to hunt out the guilty person and cleanse the city, he is speaking

60 metaphorically, but the chorus invokes the gods of vengeance and dances a wild pursuit.

On the printed page, the choral odes seem static and formal, lyric and philosophical, emotional letdowns that punctuate the series of episodes, like

65 intermissions between two acts of a play. The reader who skips the odes can get the main points of

the play. A few are worth reading as independent poems, notably the famous one in *Antigone* begin-ning, "Many are the wonders of the world, but none
70 is more wonderful than man." Some modern acting versions omit the chorus or reduce it to a few back-ground figures. Yet to the Greeks the odes were cer-tainly more than mere poetic interludes: the wild Dionysian words and movements evoked primitive
75 levels of the subconscious and at the same time served to transform primitive violence into charm and beauty and to add philosophical reflections on the meaning of human destiny.

For production today, we can only improvise
80 some partial equivalent. In Athens the entire popu-lation was familiar with choral performances. Every year each of the tribes entered a dithyramb in a con-test, rehearsing five hundred men and boys for weeks. Some modern composers have tried to write
85 dramatic music for choruses: the most notable examples are the French composer Darius Milhaud, in the primitive rhythms, shouts, and chants of his operatic version of the *Oresteia*; George Gershwin, in the Negro funeral scenes of *Porgy and Bess*; and
90 Kurt Weill, in the African choruses for *Lost in the Stars*, the musical dramatization of Alan Paton's novel, *Cry, the Beloved Country*. For revivals of Greek tragedies we have not dared use much music beyond a few phrases half shouted, half sung, and
95 drumbeats and suggestive melodies in the back-ground.

From *Invitation to the Theatre*, Copyright 1967 by George Kernodle; Harcourt, Brace, & World Inc., publisher.

THE GENERAL OUTLINE

Your quick preread of the passage should have given you a sense of its general organization:

- First Paragraph—introduces the topic of Greek tragedy
- Second Paragraph—discusses use of masks (artificial but intense)
- Third Paragraph—discusses use of chorus (also artificial but intense)
- Fourth Paragraph—expands discussion to chorus odes
- Fifth Paragraph—concludes with discussion of how Greek tragedy is performed today, and how it has influenced some modern art

And that's really all the road map you need going into the questions. Aside from that, you should take away a sense of the author's main point: Greek tragedy included many artificial devices, but these devices allowed it to rise to a high level of intensity.

You wouldn't need or even want to get more than this on your pre-reading of the passage. We know it's difficult for many students to accept, but it really is true: *Careful, detail-oriented reading does not pay on the ACT Reading test.* You just don't have the time.

> **BUILD A MENTAL ROAD MAP FOR ALL NONFICTION PASSAGES—AN OUTLINE OF THE MAJOR POINTS COVERED.**

THE FICTION AND SCIENCE PASSAGES

Now that you've learned the general approach, let's look more closely at the two kinds of ACT passage that give students the most trouble—the Prose Fiction passage and the Natural Sciences passage.

The passage breakdown for every ACT Reading test is as follows:
- Prose Fiction—one passage per test
- Nonfiction—three passages per test, one each in:
  —Social Studies
  —Natural Sciences
  —Humanities

Your approach will be essentially the same for all three nonfiction passages, since they're all well-organized essays. We've just seen how to handle passages like this. Your approach to the Prose Fiction passage, however, will be somewhat different.

The Prose Fiction Passage

The Prose Fiction passage is usually a story in which characters, fully equipped with their own motivations and emotions, interact in revealing ways. For that reason, the passage won't break down into an orderly outline or road map, so don't even try to characterize the function of each paragraph. Pay attention instead to the *story*.

> **DON'T TRY TO CONSTRUCT A MENTAL ROAD MAP FOR THE PROSE FICTION PASSAGE. INSTEAD, PAY ATTENTION TO THE STORY AND THE CHARACTERS.**

In the Prose Fiction passage, almost all the questions relate to the characters. Your job is to find the answers to the following questions:
- **Who are these people?** What are they like? How are they related to each other?
- **What is their state of mind?** Are they angry, sad, reflective, excited?
- **What's really going on?** What's happening on the surface? What's happening beneath the surface?

Most of the fiction passages focus on one person or are written from the point of view of one of the characters. Figure out who this main character is, and pay special attention to what he or she is like. Read between the lines to determine unspoken emotions and attitudes. Little hints—a momentary pause, a pointed or sarcastic comment—are sometimes all you have to go on, so pay attention. In fact, you probably want to spend more time prereading the Prose Fiction passage than you do any of the other three passages. Get a good feel for the tone and style of the passage as a whole, before going to the questions.

Fortunately, the questions for these passages tend to go more quickly than those for the other passages, so you'll be able to make up some of that lost time you spent reading the text.

> **WHEN PREREADING THE FICTION PASSAGE, ASK YOURSELF:**
> - **WHO ARE THESE PEOPLE?**
> - **WHAT IS THEIR STATE OF MIND?**
> - **WHAT'S REALLY GOING ON?**

The Natural Sciences Passage

The Science passage in the Reading subject test is often similar in outward appearance to a passage on the Science Reasoning subject test. Illustrations, graphs, and tables of information may be included. Usually, though, the emphasis in Reading is more on understanding ideas rather than reading and analyzing experiments and data.

Approaching the Science passage is not very different from approaching the other nonfiction passages, since many of those are well-organized essays laying out ideas in a straightforward, logical way.

(Though some nonfiction passages—particularly the Humanities passage—are personal essays that require a focus on the author and tone.) But you may be more likely to find unfamiliar vocabulary in Science passages. Don't panic. Any unfamiliar terms will usually be defined explicitly in the passage, or else will have definitions inferable from context.

In the Science passage, it's extremely easy to lose yourself in complex details. Don't do it. *It's especially important not to get bogged down in the Science passage!* Many students try to understand and remember everything as they read. But that's not the right ACT attitude. In your prereading of the passage, just get the gist and the outline; don't sweat the details. You'd be surprised how many questions you can answer on a passage you don't understand completely.

> **WHEN PREREADING THE SCIENCE PASSAGE, YOU MUST BE EVEN MORE CAREFUL THAN USUAL NOT TO GET BOGGED DOWN IN DETAILS.**

As you continue in your ACT training, don't forget the very first piece of Reading advice we offered: Read actively. Always know where a passage is going, and keep an eye on the structure. Use this habit whenever you read on the ACT, not just in the section called Reading. It helps on all four subject tests.

STEP 11:
READING QUESTION TYPES
AND STRATEGIES

In the first Reading step, we discussed general strategies for approaching ACT Reading, with special focus on prereading. Now let's look at the major types of *questions* you'll encounter. There are three main types of Reading question on the test: Specific Detail questions and Inference questions (which make up the bulk), and Big Picture questions (of which there are usually just a few).

The following passage is the same one you already preread. Now, however, you have the questions attached to it, so you can go through the entire process. Remember to use the three-step method:

- Preread the passage quickly.
- Consider the question stem.
- Refer to the passage (before looking at the choices).

We'll discuss selected questions from this set as examples of Specific Detail, Inference, and Big Picture questions.

Tragedy was the invention of the Greeks. In their Golden Age, the fifth century before Christ, they produced the world's greatest dramatists, new forms of tragedy and comedy that have been models ever 5 since, and a theatre that every age goes back to for rediscovery of some basic principles. . . .

Since it derived from primitive religious rites, with masks and ceremonial costumes, and made use of music, dance, and poetry, the Greek drama 10 was at the opposite pole from the modern realistic stage. In fact, probably no other theatre in history has made fuller use of the intensities of art. The masks, made of painted linen, wood, and plaster, brought down from primitive days the atmosphere 15 of gods, heroes, and demons. Our nineteenth-and twentieth-century grandfathers thought masks must have been very artificial. Today, however, we appreciate their exciting intensity and can see that in a large theatre they were indispensable. If they 20 allowed no fleeting change of expression during a single episode, they could give for each episode in turn more intense expression than any human face could. When Oedipus comes back with bleeding eyes, the new mask could be more terrible than any 25 facial makeup the audience could endure, yet in its sculpted intensity more beautiful than a real face.

Most essential of all intensities, and hardest for us to understand, was the chorus. Yet many playwrights today are trying to find some equivalent to 30 do for a modern play what the chorus did for the Greeks. During the episodes played by the actors, the chorus would only provide a background of group response, enlarging and reverberating the

emotions of the actors, sometimes protesting and
35 opposing but in general serving as ideal spectators
to stir and lead the reactions of the audience. But
between episodes, with the actors out of the way,
the chorus took over. We have only the words, not
the music or dance, and some translations of the
40 odes are in such formal, old-fashioned language
that it is hard to guess that they were accompanied
by vigorous, sometimes even wild dances and symbolic actions that filled an orchestra which in some
cities was sixty to ninety feet in diameter.
45 Sometimes the chorus expressed simple horror or
lament. Sometimes it chanted and acted out, in unison and in precise formations of rows and lines, the
acts of violence the characters were enacting offstage. When Phaedra rushes offstage in *Hippolytus*
50 to hang herself from the rafters, the members of
the chorus, all fifteen of them, perform in mime and
chant the act of tying the rope and swinging from
the rafters. Sometimes the chorus tells or reenacts
an incident of history or legend that throws light on
55 the situation in the play. Sometimes the chorus
puts into specific action what is a general intention
in the mind of the main character. When Oedipus
resolves to hunt out the guilty person and cleanse
the city, he is speaking metaphorically, but the cho-
60 rus invokes the gods of vengeance and dances a
wild pursuit.

On the printed page, the choral odes seem static and formal, lyric and philosophical, emotional letdowns that punctuate the series of episodes, like
65 intermissions between two acts of a play. The reader who skips the odes can get the main points of

the play. A few are worth reading as independent poems, notably the famous one in *Antigone* begin-
ning, "Many are the wonders of the world, but none
70 is more wonderful than man." Some modern acting
versions omit the chorus or reduce it to a few back-
ground figures. Yet to the Greeks the odes were certainly more than mere poetic interludes: the wild
Dionysian words and movements evoked primitive
75 levels of the subconscious and at the same time
served to transform primitive violence into charm
and beauty and to add philosophical reflections on
the meaning of human destiny.

For production today, we can only improvise
80 some partial equivalent. In Athens the entire population was familiar with choral performances. Every
year each of the tribes entered a dithyramb in a con-
test, rehearsing five hundred men and boys for
weeks. Some modern composers have tried to write
85 dramatic music for choruses: the most notable
examples are the French composer Darius Milhaud,
in the primitive rhythms, shouts, and chants of his
operatic version of the *Oresteia*; George Gershwin,
in the Negro funeral scenes of *Porgy and Bess*; and
90 Kurt Weill, in the African choruses for *Lost in the
Stars*, the musical dramatization of Alan Paton's
novel, *Cry, the Beloved Country*. For revivals of
Greek tragedies we have not dared use much music
beyond a few phrases half shouted, half sung, and
95 drumbeats and suggestive melodies in the back-
ground.

From *Invitation to the Theatre*, © 1967 by George Kernodle; Harcourt, Brace, & World Inc., publisher.

Step 11: Reading Question Types and Strategies

1. Combined with the passage's additional information, the fact that some Greek orchestras were sixty to ninety feet across suggests that:

    A. few spectators were able to see the stage.

    B. no one performer could dominate a performance.

    C. choruses and masks helped overcome the distance between actors and audience.

    D. Greek tragedies lacked the emotional force of modern theatrical productions.

2. Which of the following claims expresses the writer's opinion and not a fact?

    F. The Greek odes contained Dionysian words and movements.

    G. Greek theater has made greater use of the intensities of art than has any other theater in history.

    H. Many modern playwrights are trying to find an equivalent to the Greek chorus.

    J. The chorus was an essential part of Greek tragedy.

3. The description of the chorus's enactment of Phaedra's offstage suicide (lines 49–53) shows that, in contrast to modern theater, ancient Greek theater was:

    A. more violent.

    B. more concerned with satisfying an audience.

    C. more apt to be historically accurate.

    D. less concerned with a realistic portrayal of events.

Part Four: The ACT Reading Test

4. It can be inferred that one consequence of the Greeks' use of masks was that:

   F. the actors often had to change masks between episodes.

   G. the characters in the play could not convey emotion.

   H. the actors wearing masks played nonspeaking roles.

   J. good acting ability was not important to the Greeks.

5. Which of the following is supported by the information in the second paragraph (lines 7–26)?

   A. Masks in Greek drama combined artistic beauty with emotional intensity.

   B. The use of masks in Greek drama was better appreciated in the nineteenth century than it is now.

   C. Masks in Greek drama were used to portray gods but never human beings.

   D. Contemporary scholars seriously doubt the importance of masks to Greek theater.

6. The author indicates in lines 58–59 that Oedipus's resolution "to hunt out the guilty person and cleanse the city" was:

   F. at odds with what he actually does later in the performance.

   G. misinterpreted by the chorus.

   H. dramatized by the actions of the chorus.

   J. angrily condemned by the chorus.

KAPLAN

Step 11: Reading Question Types and Strategies

7. According to the passage, when actors were present on stage, the chorus would:

    A. look on as silently as spectators.

    B. inevitably agree with the actors' actions.

    C. communicate to the audience solely through mime.

    D. react to the performance as an audience might.

8. The main point of the fourth paragraph (lines 62–78) is that choral odes:

    F. should not be performed by modern choruses.

    G. have a meaning and beauty that are lost in modern adaptations.

    H. can be safely ignored by a modern-day reader.

    J. are worthwhile only in *Antigone*.

9. The passage suggests that modern revivals of Greek tragedies "have not dared use much music" (line 93) because:

    A. modern instruments would appear out of place.

    B. to do so would require a greater understanding of how choral odes were performed.

    C. music would distract the audience from listening to the words of choral odes.

    D. such music is considered far too primitive for modern audiences.

10. *Porgy and Bess* and *Lost in the Stars* are modern plays that:

    F. are revivals of Greek tragedies.

    G. use music to evoke the subconscious.

    H. perform primitive Greek music.

    J. have made use of musical choruses.

THE GENERAL OUTLINE

- First Paragraph—introduces the topic of Greek tragedy
- Second Paragraph—discusses use of masks (artificial but intense)
- Third Paragraph—discusses use of chorus (also artificial but intense)
- Fourth Paragraph—expands discussion to chorus odes
- Fifth Paragraph—concludes with discussion of how Greek tragedy is performed today, and how it has influenced some modern art

Don't forget to phrase in your mind the author's main point: Greek tragedy included many artificial devices, but these devices allowed it to rise to a high level of intensity.

SPECIFIC DETAIL QUESTIONS

Questions 6 and 7 above are typical Detail questions. As you've seen, some Detail questions (such as 6) give you a line reference to help you out; others (such as 7) don't, forcing you either to start tearing your hair out (if you're an unprepared test taker) or else to seek out the answer based on your own sense of how the passage is laid out (one of the two key reasons to preread the passage). With either type of Detail question, once you've found the part of the passage that a question refers to, the answer is often (though not always) pretty obvious.

ALWAYS REFER TO THE PASSAGE BEFORE ANSWERING A QUESTION.

Question 6 provides a line reference (lines 58–59), but to answer the question confidently, you should have also read a few lines before and a few lines after the cited lines. There you would have read: "Sometimes the chorus puts into action what is a general intention in the mind of the main character. When Oedipus resolves. . . ." Clearly, the Oedipus example is meant to illustrate the point about the chorus acting out a character's intentions. So H is correct—it is "dramatizing" (or acting out) Oedipus's resolution. (By the way, G might have been tempting, but there's no real evidence that the chorus is "misinterpreting," just that it's "putting a general intention into specific action.")

Question 7 is a Detail question *without* a line reference. Such questions are common on the ACT. This question's mention of the chorus should have sent you to Paragraph 3, but that's a long paragraph, so you probably had to skim it to find the answer in lines 31–36, where the author claims that the chorus serves to "lead the reactions of the audience"—captured by correct choice D.

WHEN GIVEN A SPECIFIC LINE REFERENCE, ALWAYS READ A FEW SENTENCES BEFORE AND AFTER THE CITED LINES, TO GET A SENSE OF THE CONTEXT.

INFERENCE QUESTIONS

For Inference questions, your job is to combine ideas logically to make an inference—something that's not stated explicitly in the passage but that is definitely said *im*plicitly. Often, Inference questions have a word like *suggest, infer, inference,* or *imply* in the question stem to tip you off.

To succeed on these, you have to "read between the lines." Common sense is your best tool here. You use various bits of information in the passage as evidence for your own logical conclusion.

Like Detail Questions, Inference Questions only sometimes contain line references. Question 9 does, referring you to line 93, but you really have to keep the context of the entire paragraph in mind when you make your inference. Why would modern revivals not have "dared" to use much music? Well, the paragraph opens by saying that modern productions "can only improvise some partial equivalent" to the choral odes. Inferably, since we can only improvise the odes, we don't understand very much about them. That's why the use of music would be considered daring, and why choice B is correct.

Question 4 provides no line reference, but the mention of masks should have sent you to the second paragraph of the passage, where (according to your trusty road map) masks are discussed. Lines 20–21 explain that masks "allowed no fleeting change of expression during a single episode." Treat that as your first piece of evidence. Your second comes in lines 21–23: "[T]hey [the masks] could give for each episode in turn more intense expression than any human face could." Put those two pieces of evidence together—masks can't change expression during a *single* episode, but they can give expression for each episode *in turn.*

Clearly, the actors must have changed masks between episodes, so that they could express the different emotions that different episodes required. Choice F is correct.

> **MAKING INFERENCES REQUIRES THAT YOU COMBINE BITS OF INFORMATION FROM DIFFERENT PARTS OF THE PASSAGE.**

One warning: Be careful to keep your inferences as "close" to the passage as possible. Don't make wild inferential leaps. An inference should seem to follow naturally and inevitably from the evidence provided in the passage.

> **DON'T MAKE YOUR INFERENCES TOO EXTREME.**

BIG PICTURE QUESTIONS

There are a few questions on the Reading section that test your understanding of the theme, purpose, and organization of the passage. For these Big Picture questions, your main task is different from what it is for Detail or Inference questions, though you should still plan to find the answer in the passages. Big Picture questions tend to focus on:

- The main point or purpose of a passage or part of a passage
- The author's attitude or tone
- The logic underlying the author's argument
- How ideas in different parts of the passage relate to each other
- The difference between fact and opinion

One way to see the Big Picture is to read actively. As you read, ask yourself, "What's the point of this? Why is the author saying this?"

IF YOU'RE STILL STUMPED AFTER READING THE PASSAGE, TRY
DOING THE DETAIL AND INFERENCE QUESTIONS FIRST—TO
HELP YOU FILL IN THE BIG PICTURE.

Question 8 asks for the main idea of a particular paragraph—
namely, the fourth, which our general outline indicates as the paragraph about choral odes. Skimming that paragraph, you find reference to how the odes seem to us modern people—"static and formal" (lines 62–63), "like intermissions between two acts of a play"
(lines 64–65). Later, the author states, by way of contrast (note the
use of the clue word *yet*): "Yet to the Greeks the odes were certainly more than mere poetic interludes" (lines 72–73). Clearly, the
author in this paragraph wants to contrast our modern static view
of the odes with the Greeks' view of them as something more. That
idea is best captured by choice G.

Question 2, meanwhile, is another common type of Big Picture
question—one that requires that you distinguish between expressions of fact and opinion in the passage. A simple test for fact (ver-
sus opinion) is this: Can it be proven objectively? If yes, it's a fact.

The content of Greek odes (choice F) is a matter of fact; you can go
to a Greek ode and find out whether it does or doesn't contain
Dionysian words. Similarly, the efforts of modern playwrights to
find an equivalent to the Greek chorus (choice H), and the central
importance of the chorus to Greek tragedy (choice J) can be factually verified.

But the "intensities of art" are a subjective matter. What one person
thinks is intense might strike another as simply boring. So G is the
expression of opinion the question is looking for.

KAPLAN

Step 11: Reading Question Types and Strategies

FIND AND PARAPHRASE

The examples above show that your real task in Reading is different from what you might expect. Your main job is to *find* the answers. In other words, "find and paraphrase." But students tend to think that their task in Reading is to "comprehend and remember." That's the wrong mindset.

Here's a key to the Greek tragedy passage, so that you can check the answers to the questions not discussed above.

	ANSWER	REFER TO	TYPE	COMMENTS
		(NONFICTION—HUMANITIES)		
1.	C	Lines 11–20, 40–46	Inference	Q-stem emphasizes distance between audience and stage; masks and choruses help to "enlarge" the action, so that it can be understood from a distance.
2.	G	Throughout	Big Picture	Discussed above.
3.	D	Lines 48–51	Inference	Combine info from lines 7–15, 48–51, 70–76.
4.	F	Lines 20–23	Inference	Discussed above.
5.	A	Lines 7–26	Inference	Combine info from lines 22–26, 10–12, 19–22.
6.	H	Lines 57–59	Detail	Discussed above.
7.	D	Lines 31–36	Detail	Discussed above.
8.	G	Lines 62–65	Big Picture	Discussed above.
9.	B	Lines 93–95	Inference	Discussed above.
10.	J	Lines 84–96	Detail	"Some modern composers have tried to write dramatic music for choruses." (lines 84–85)

SKIPPING

Now that you've done a full-length passage and questions, you've probably encountered at least a few questions that you found unanswerable. What do you do if you can't find the answer in the passage, or if you *can* find it but don't understand, or if you *do* understand but can't see an answer choice that makes sense? Skip the question. Skipping is probably more important in Reading than in any other ACT question type. Many students find it useful to skip as many as half of the questions on the first pass through a set of Reading questions. That's fine.

> **ANSWER THE EASY QUESTIONS FOR EACH PASSAGE FIRST.**
> **SKIP THE TOUGH ONES AND COME BACK TO THEM LATER.**

When you come back to a Reading question the second time, it usually makes sense to use the process of elimination. The first time around, you tried to find the *right* answer but you couldn't. So, now try to identify the three *wrong* answers. Eliminating three choices is slower than finding one right choice, so don't make it your main strategy for Reading. But it's a good way to try a second attack on a question.

Another thing to consider when attacking a question for a second time is that the right answer may have been hidden. Maybe it's written in an unexpected way, with different vocabulary. Or maybe there is another good way to answer the question that you haven't thought of. But remember not to get bogged down when you come back to a question. Be willing to admit that there are some problems you just can't answer. Guess if you have to.

THE ACT SCIENCE REASONING TEST

STEP 12:
BASIC SCIENCE TECHNIQUES

Many ACT takers worry about "not knowing enough science" to do well on the science reasoning test. But the fact of the matter is, you really don't need to be a science whiz to do well on the ACT. Knowing science is a plus, of course, and it certainly can help your work in the science reasoning subject test. But you don't need to know a truckload of scientific facts to answer these science questions. The questions are answerable from the information in the passage.

READING SKILLS AND "READING" SKILLS

ACT Science Reasoning requires many of the same skills that ACT Reading does. The difference between Reading and Science Reasoning, however, is that the "details" you have to find in the Science Reasoning passages almost all relate to numbers or scientific processes or both, and they are often contained in graphs and tables rather than in paragraph form. The secret to finding most of these details is:

- **Learn to "read" graphs, tables, and research summaries.**
  Some questions involve only accurately retrieving data from a single graph or table, while others involve combining

knowledge from two graphs or tables. Still others involve understanding experimental methods well enough to evaluate information.

- **Learn to look for patterns in the numbers that appear.** Do these numbers get bigger or smaller? Where are the highest numbers? Where are the lowest? At what point do the numbers change? A little calculation is sometimes required, but not much. In Science Reasoning, you won't be computing with numbers so much as thinking about what they mean.

KAPLAN'S THREE-STEP METHOD

In Science Reasoning, you have 35 minutes to complete seven short passages. Each passage with questions should average five minutes. We recommend using just about one minute to preread, and then a total of about four minutes to consider the questions and refer to the passage (that's about 40 seconds per question). Here's a three-step method that you can use as a guide for attacking passages in the Science Reasoning section:

STEP 1: Preread the Passage

It's especially important in Science Reasoning not to get bogged down in the details. Some of the material covered is extremely technical, and you'll just get frustrated trying to understand it completely. So it's crucial that you skim, to get a general idea of what's going on and—just as important—to get a sense of where certain types of data can be found.

Almost all Science Reasoning passages have the same basic structure. They begin with an introduction. Always read through the introduction first to orient yourself and get a sense of the overall situation.

After reading the introduction, quickly scan the rest of the passage. How is the information presented? Graphs? Diagrams? Are there experiments? What seems to be important? Size? Shape? Temperature? Speed? Chemical composition? Don't worry about details and don't try to remember it all. Plan to refer to the passage when answering the questions. Remember, your goal is to answer questions, NOT to learn and remember everything that goes on in the passage.

> **DON'T WORRY ABOUT DETAILS ON YOUR INITIAL READ-THROUGH.**

STEP 2: Consider the Question Stem

Most of your time in Science Reasoning will be spent considering questions and referring to the passage to find the answers. Here's where you should do most of your really careful reading. It's essential that you understand exactly what the question is asking. Then, go back to the passage and get a sense of what the answer should be *before* looking at the choices.

STEP 3: Refer to the Passage

You have to be diligent about referring to the passage. Your preread should have given you an idea of where particular kinds of data can be found. Sometimes the questions themselves will direct you to the right place.

Be careful not to mix up units when taking information from graphs, tables, and summaries. Make sure you don't confuse opposites. The difference between a correct and an incorrect answer will often be a "*de*crease" where an "*in*crease" should be. Always look for words like *not* and *except* in the questions.

> **ALWAYS REFER TO THE PASSAGE AND THE QUESTION STEM BEFORE SELECTING AN ANSWER.**

READING TABLES AND GRAPHS

Most of the specific information in ACT Science Reasoning passages is contained in tables or graphs, usually accompanied by explanatory material. *Knowing how to read data from tables and graphs is critical to success on the Science Reasoning subject test!*

In order to read most graphs and tables, you have to do four things:
- Determine what is being represented.
- Determine what the axes (or columns and rows) represent.
- Take note of units of measurement.
- Look for trends in the data.

Let's say you saw the following graph in a Science Reasoning passage:

Step 12: Basic Science Techniques

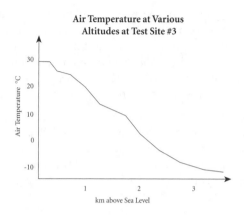

Air Temperature at Various
Altitudes at Test Site #3

- **Determine what is being represented.** Most graphs and tables have titles that tell you what they represent. For some, though, you may have to get that information from the introduction. Here, the graph is representing how cold or hot the air is at various altitudes at Test Site #3.
- **Determine what the axes represent.** These, too, are usually labeled. In this graph, the *x*-axis represents kilometers above sea level, while the *y*-axis represents the air temperature in degrees Celsius.
- **Take note of units of measurement.** Note that distance here is measured in *kilometers*, not miles or feet. Temperature is measured in degrees *Celsius*, not Fahrenheit.
- **Look for trends in the data.** The "pattern" of the data in this graph is pretty clear. As you rise in altitude, the temperature drops—the higher the altitude, the lower the temperature.

The sloping line on the graph represents the various temperatures measured at the various altitudes. To find what the measured temperature was at, say, 2 km above sea level, find the 2 km point on the x-axis and trace your finger directly up from it until it hits the line. It does so at about the level of 3° C. In other words, at an altitude of 2 km above sea level at Test Site #3, the air temperature was about 3° C.

You should follow a similar procedure with tables of information. For instance, in the introduction to the passage in which the following table might have appeared, you would have learned that scientists were trying to determine the effects of two pollutants (Pb and Hg, lead and mercury) on the trout populations of a particular river.

Location	Water temperature (°C)	Presence of Pb (parts per million)	Presence of Hg (parts per million)	Population Density of Speckled Trout (# per 100 m³)	Population Density of Brown Trout (# per 100 m³)
1	15.4	0	3	5.5	7.9
2	16.1	0	1	12.2	3.5
3	16.3	1	67	0	0
4	15.8	54	3	15.3	5.7
5	16.0	2	4	24	9.5

- **Determine what is being represented.** There's no informative title for this table, but the introduction would have told you what the table represents.
- **Determine what the columns and rows represent.** In tables, you get columns and rows instead of x- and y-axes. But the principle is the same. Here, each row represents the data from a different numbered location on the river. Each column represents different data—water temperature, presence of the first pollutant, presence of the second pollutant, population of one kind of trout, population of another kind of trout.
- **Take note of units of measurement.** Temperature is measured in Celsius. The two pollutants are measured in parts-per-million (or ppm). The trout populations are measured in number per 100 cubic meters of river.
- **Look for trends in the data.** Glancing at the table, it looks like locations where the Hg concentration is high (as in Location 3), the trout population is virtually nonexistent. This would seem to indicate that trout life and a high Hg concentration are incompatible. But notice the location where the other pollutant is abundant—in Location 4. Here, both trout populations seem to be more in line with other locations. That would seem to indicate that this other pollutant—Pb—is NOT as detrimental to trout populations as Hg is.

LOOK FOR PATTERNS AND TRENDS

When you first examine a graph or table, don't focus on exact numbers. Look for *patterns* in the numbers. Don't assume that there is always a pattern or trend. Finding that there isn't a pattern is just as important as finding that there is one. Let's look at the three characteristic patterns in graphs and tables.

Extremes

Extremes—or maximums and minimums—are merely the highest and lowest points that things reach. In tables, the minimums and maximums will be represented by especially high and low numbers. In graphs, they will be represented by high and low x- and y-coordinates. In bar charts, they will be represented by the tallest and shortest bars.

In discussing the extremes in the trout populations table, we saw how isolating the locations at which trout populations and chemical concentrations were at their maximum and minimum values led us to a conclusion about the compatibility of trout and water containing high concentrations of Hg.

Critical Points

Critical points—or points of change—are values at which something dramatic happens. For example, at atmospheric pressure water freezes at $0°$ C and boils at about $100°$ C. If you examined water at various temperatures below the lower of these two critical points, it would be solid. If you examined water at various temperatures between the two points, it would be liquid. If you examined water above the higher critical point, it would be a gas.

When you scan the numbers in a chart or points on a graph, look for places where values bunch together, where an increasing trend switches to a decreasing trend, or where suddenly something special happens. At atmosphere pressure, $0°$ C is a critical point for water— as is $100°$ C—since something special happens: The substance changes form.

To find out how critical points can help you evaluate data, let's look at a graph representing the concentration of *E. coli* (a common type of bacterium) in a location called Cooling Pool B.

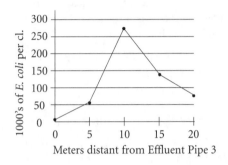

Notice how the concentration is low very near Effluent Pipe 3. From there, it rises until about 10 meters away from the pipe, then it falls again, tapering off the farther you get from the pipe. There's a critical point, then, right around 10 meters from Effluent Pipe 3. Somehow, that vicinity is most conducive to the growth of *E. coli*. As you move closer to or farther away from that point, the concentration falls off. So, in looking to explain the data, you'd want to focus on that location—10 meters from the pipe. What is it about that location that's so special? Why is it that more *E. coli* grows there?

Variation

Variation is a bit more complex than extremes or critical points. Variation refers to the way two different things change *in relation to each other*. Direct variation means that two things vary in the same way: When one gets bigger, the other does too; when one gets smaller, so does the other. Inverse variation means that two things vary in *opposite* ways: When one gets bigger the other gets smaller, and vice versa. We saw an example of inverse variation in the air temperature graph, in which altitude and air temperature varied inversely—as altitude *in*creased, air temperature *de*creased. Observing this inverse variation allowed us to make conclusions about the relationship between altitude and air temperature.

When reading data, you should be on the lookout for the three characteristic patterns or trends:
- Extremes (maximums and minimums)
- Critical points (or points of change)
- Direct or inverse variation (or proportionality)

To do well on Science Reasoning, you have to be able to read graphs and tables, paying special attention to trends and patterns in the data. And sometimes, that's all you need to do to get most of the points on a passage.

STEP 13:
EXPERIMENTS

In Step 12, you learned that to succeed on the ACT Science Reasoning test, you must be able to spot trends and patterns in the data of graphs and tables. But that's not all that you need to do well. You should also learn how to think like a scientist. You don't have to *know* very much science (although it certainly helps), but you should at least be familiar with how scientists go about getting and testing knowledge.

HOW SCIENTISTS THINK

Scientists use two very different kinds of logic, which (to keep things nontechnical) we'll call:
- General-to-Specific Thinking
- Specific-to-General Thinking

General-to-Specific

In some cases, scientists have already discovered a law of nature and wish to apply their knowledge to a specific case. For example, a scientist may wish to know how fast a pebble (call it Pebble A) will be falling when it hits the ground three seconds after being dropped. There is a law of physics that says on Earth, falling objects accelerate at a rate of about 9.8 m/sec^2. The scientist could use this known general law to calculate the specific information she needs: After three seconds, the object would be falling at a rate of about 3 sec × 9.8 m/sec^2, or roughly 30 m/sec. You could think of this kind of logic as *general-to-specific*. The scientist uses a *general* rule (the acceleration of any object falling on Earth) to find a *specific* fact (the speed of Pebble A).

Specific-to-General

But scientists use a different kind of thinking in order to discover new laws of nature. In these cases, they examine many facts and then draw a general conclusion about what they've seen. For example, a scientist might watch hundreds of different kinds of frogs live and die, and might notice that all of them developed from tadpoles. She might then announce a theory: All frogs develop from tadpoles. You could think of this kind of logic as specific-to-general. The scientist looks at many specific frogs to arrive at general rule about all frogs.

This conclusion is called a "hypothesis," not a fact or a "truth," because the scientist has not checked every single frog in the universe. She knows that theoretically there *could* be a frog somewhere that grows, say, from pond scum or from a Dalmatian puppy. But until she finds such a frog, it is reasonable to think that her theory is correct. Many hypotheses, in fact, are so well documented that they become the equivalent of laws of nature.

> **FOR SCIENCE REASONING QUESTIONS, ASK YOURSELF WHETHER YOU SHOULD BE DOING GENERAL-TO-SPECIFIC OR SPECIFIC-TO-GENERAL THINKING.**

In your science classes in school, you mostly learn about general-to-specific thinking. Your teachers explain general rules of science to you and then expect you to apply these rules to solve problems. Some ACT Science Reasoning questions are like that, too, but most are not. Most of the questions on the ACT test specific-to-general thinking. They test your ability to see the kinds of patterns in specific data that, as a scientist, you would use to formulate your own general hypotheses. We did something like this in Step 12, when we theorized—based on the trends we found in a table of data—that the pollutant Hg was in some way detrimental to trout populations.

HOW EXPERIMENTS WORK

Many ACT passages describe experiments and expect you to understand how they're designed. Experiments help scientists do specific-to-general thinking in a reliable and efficient way. Consider the tadpole researcher above. In a real-world situation, she would probably notice that some frogs develop from tadpoles and wonder if maybe they all did. Then she'd know what to look for and could check many frogs systematically. This process contains the two basic steps of any experiment:

- Form a Hypothesis (guessing that all frogs come from tadpoles), and
- Test a Hypothesis (checking frogs to see if this guess was right).

Scientists are often interested in cause-and-effect relationships. Having formed her hypothesis about tadpoles, a scientist might wonder what causes a tadpole to become a frog, for instance. To test causal relationships, a special kind of experiment is needed. She must test one possible cause at a time in order to isolate which one actually produces the effect in question. For example, the scientist might inject tadpoles with several kinds of hormones. Some of these tadpoles might die. Others might grow into frogs normally. But a few—those injected with Hormone X, say—might remain tadpoles for an indefinite time. One reasonable explanation is that

Hormone X in some way inhibited whatever causes normal frog development. In other words, the scientist would hypothesize a causal relationship between Hormone X and frog development.

Watch Your Tadpoles' Diets

The relationship between Hormone X and frog development, however, would not be demonstrated very well if the scientist also fed different diets to different tadpoles, kept some in warmer water, or allowed some to have more room to swim than others—or if she didn't also watch tadpoles that were injected with no hormones at all but that were otherwise were kept under the same conditions as the treated tadpoles. Why? Because if the "eternal tadpoles" had a diet that differed from that of the others, the scientist wouldn't know whether it was Hormone X or the special diet that kept the eternal tadpoles from becoming frogs. Moreover, if their water was warmer than that of the others, maybe it was the warmth that somehow kept the tadpoles from developing. And if she didn't watch untreated tadpoles (a "control group"), she couldn't be sure whether, under the same conditions, a normal, untreated tadpole would also remain undeveloped.

Thus, a scientist creating a well-designed experiment will:
- Ensure that there's a single variable (like Hormone X) that varies from test to test, or group to group.
- Ensure that all other factors (diet, temperatures, space, etcetera) remain the same.
- Ensure that there is a control group (tadpoles who don't get any Hormone X at all) for comparison purposes.

Find What Varies

One advantage to knowing how experiments work is that *you can tell what a researcher is trying to find out about by checking to see what she allows to vary.* That is what's being researched—in this case, Hormone X. Data about things other than hormones and tadpole-to-frog development would be outside the design of the experiment. Information about other factors might be interesting, but could not be part of a scientific proof.

For example, if some of the injected tadpoles that did grow into frogs later turned into princes, the data about the hormone they were given would not prove what causes frogs to become princes. However, the data could be used to design another experiment intended to explore what could make a frog into a prince.

Whenever you see an experiment in Science Reasoning, therefore, ask yourself three things:

1. What's the factor that's being varied?—That is what's being tested.
2. What's the control group?—It's the group that has nothing special done to it.
3. What do the results show?—What differences exist between the results for the control group and those for the other group(s)? Or between the results for one treated group and those for another, differently treated group?

WHEN ANALYZING EXPERIMENTS, ASK YOURSELF:
• WHAT FACTOR IS BEING VARIED?
• WHAT'S THE CONTROL GROUP?
• WHAT DO THE RESULTS SHOW?

HANDLING EXPERIMENT QUESTIONS

On the next page is a full-fledged Science Reasoning passage organized around two experiments. Use the three-step method (preread the passage, consider the question stem, refer to the passage before looking at the choices), but this time, since this is a passage that centers on experiments, remember to ask yourself the three questions above. Take five or six minutes to do the passage and its questions.

Passage II

A *mutualistic* relationship between two species increases the chances of growth or survival for both of them. Several species of fungi form mutualistic relationships called *mycorrhizae* with the roots of plants. The benefits to each species are shown in the figure below.

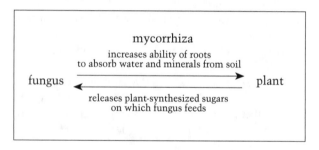

Some of the plant species that require or benefit from the presence of mycorrhizal fungi are noted below.

Cannot survive without mycorrhizae	Grow better with mycorrhizae
All conifers Some deciduous trees (e.g. birch, beech) Orchids	Citrus trees Ericaceae (heath, rhododendrons, azaleas) Grapes Soybeans

Agronomists investigated the effects of mycorrhizae on plant growth and survival in the following studies.

Study 1

Three 4-acre plots were prepared with soil from a pine forest. The soil for Plot A was mixed with substantial quantities of cultured mycorrhizal fungi. The soil for Plot B contained only naturally occurring mycorrhizal fungi. The soil for Plot C was sterilized in order to kill any mycorrhizal fungi. Additionally, Plot C was lined with concrete. After planting, Plot C was covered with a fabric that filtered out microorganisms while permitting air and light to penetrate, as shown below. Two hundred-fifty pine seedlings were planted in each of the three plots. All plots were treated to the same environmental conditions. The six-month survival rates were recorded in the table below.

	# Seedlings alive after 6 months	Utilization of available K (average)	Utilization of available P (average)
Plot A	107	18%	62%
Plot B	34	10%	13%
Plot C	0	N/A	N/A

N/A = not applicable

Study 2

The roots of surviving seedlings from Plots A and B were analyzed to determine how efficiently they absorbed potassium (K) and phosphorus (P) from the soil. The results were added to the table above.

1. The most likely purpose of the concrete liner was:

   A. to block the seedlings from sending out taproots to water below the plot.

   B. to prevent mycorrhizal fungi in the surrounding soil from colonizing the plot.

   C. to absorb potassium and phosphorus from the soil for later analysis.

   D. to provide a firm foundation for mycorrhizal fungi in the plot.

2. Mycorrhizae are highly susceptible to acid rain. Given
    the information from the passage, acid rain is probably
    most harmful to:

    F. wheat fields.

    G. birch forests.

    H. orange groves.

    J. grape vines.

3. In a third study, pine seedlings were planted in soil
    from a different location. The soil was prepared as in
    Study 1. This time, the survival rates for seedlings
    planted in Plot A and Plot B were almost identical to
    each other. Which of the following theories would NOT
    help to explain these results?

    A. Sterilization killed all the naturally occurring mycorrhizal fungi
       in the new soil.

    B. The new soil was so mineral deficient that it could not sustain
       life.

    C. The new soil was naturally more fertile than that used in
       Study 1.

    D. Large quantities of mycorrhizal fungi occurred naturally in
       the new soil.

4. According to the passage, in which of the following ways do plants benefit from mycorrhizal associations?

    I.   More efficient sugar production
    II. Enhanced ability to survive drought
    III. Increased mineral absorption

    F. I only

    G. III only

    H. II and III only

    J. I, II, and III

5. Which of the following generalizations is supported by the results of Study 2?

    A. Mycorrhizal fungi are essential for the survival of pine seedlings.

    B. Growth rates for pine seedlings may be improved by adding mycorrhizal fungi to the soil.

    C. Mycorrhizal fungi contain minerals that are not normally found in pine forest soil.

    D. Pine seedlings cannot absorb all the potassium that is present in the soil.

(A) (B) (C) (D)

ANSWERS: 1. B, 2. G, 3. A, 4. H, 5. D

A Beneficial Fungus

Notice how many diagrams and tables were used here. That's common in experiment passages, where information is given to you in a wide variety of forms. Typically, however, the experiments themselves are clearly labeled, as Study 1 and Study 2 were here.

A quick prereading of the introduction would have revealed the topic of the experiments here—the "mutualistic relationship" between some fungi and some plant roots, the relationship called *mycorrhiza* ("myco" for short). The first diagram just shows you who gets what out of this relationship. The benefit accruing to the plant (the arrow pointing to the word *plant*) is an increased ability to absorb water and minerals. The benefit accruing to the fungus (the other arrow) is the plant-synthesized sugars on which the fungus feeds. That's the mutual benefit the myco association creates.

Notice, by the way, that reading this first diagram alone is enough to answer Question 4, which we'll do right now. The question is asking, essentially, what do the plants get out of the association? And we just answered that: increased ability to absorb water and minerals. Statement III is obviously correct, but so is Statement II, since increased water absorption would indeed enhance the plant's ability to survive drought (a drought is a shortage of water, after all). Statement I, though, is a distortion. We know that the fungi benefit from sugars produced by the plants, but we don't have any evidence that the association actually causes plants to produce sugar more efficiently. So I is out; II and III are in, making H the answer to Question 4.

Can't Live Without Those Fungi

But let's get back to the passage. We've just learned who gets what out of the myco association. Now we get a chart that shows what *kind* of plants enter into such associations. Some (those in the first column) are so dependent on myco associations that they can't live without them. Others (those in the second column) merely grow better with them; presumably they could live without them.

Here again, there's a question we can answer based solely on information in this one table. Question 2 tells us that mycos are highly susceptible to acid rain, and then asks what kind of plant communities would be most harmed by acid rain. Well, if acid rain hurts mycos, then the plants that are most dependent on myco fungi (that is, the ones listed in the first column) would be the most harmed by acid rain. Of the four choices, only birch forests, choice G, corresponds to something in column 1 of the table. Birch trees can't even survive without myco fungi, so anything that hurts myco fungi would inferrably hurt birch forests. (Grape vines and orange groves—which are citrus trees—would also be hurt by acid rain, but not as much, since they can survive without myco fungi. We're told nothing about wheat in the passage.)

Well, we've answered two of the five questions already and we haven't even gotten to the first experiment. That brings up an important point—namely, that even in passages that center around experiments, there are plenty of Data Analysis questions.

> **IF TIME IS A PROBLEM, FOCUS ON THE QUESTIONS THAT JUST REQUIRE ANALYZING DATA FROM A SINGLE TABLE OR GRAPH.**

Don't expect there to be passages that have only Data Analysis questions, other passages that have only Experiment questions, and others that have only Principle questions. Most passages will have a mixture of all three.

Study 1

Now look at the first experiment. Three plots, each with differently treated soil, are planted with pine seedlings. Plot A gets soil with cultivated myco fungi; Plot B gets untreated soil with only naturally occurring myco fungi; and Plot C gets no myco fungi at all, since the soil has been sterilized and isolated (via the concrete lining and the fabric covering). Now ask yourself the three important experiment questions:

- What factor is being varied?
  The factor being varied is the amount of myco fungi in the soil. Plot A gets a lot; Plot B gets just the normal amount; Plot C gets none at all. It's clear, then, that the scientists are testing the effects of myco fungi on the growth of pine seedlings.
- What's the control group?
  The plants in Plot B, since they get untreated soil. To learn the effects of the fungi, then, the scientists will compare the results from fungi-rich Plot A with the control, and the results from fungi-poor Plot C with the same control.
- What do the results show?
  The results are listed in the first column of the table below the illustration of Plot C. And they are decisive: No seedlings at all survived in Plot C; 34 did in Plot B; and 107 did in Plot A. The minimums and maximums coincide. Minimum fungi = minimum number of surviving

seedlings; maximum fungi = maximum number of surviving seedlings. Clearly there's a cause-and-effect relationship here. Myco fungi probably help pine seedlings survive.

Questions 1 and 3 can be answered solely on the basis of Study 1. Question 1 is merely a procedural question: Why the concrete liner in Plot C? Well, in the analysis of the experiment above, we saw that the factor being varied was amount of myco fungi. Plot C was designed to have none at all. It follows, then, that the concrete liner was probably there to prevent any stray myco fungi from entering the sterilized soil—choice B.

Question 3 actually sets up an extra experiment based on Study 1. The soils were prepared in the same way, except that the soil came from a different location. The results? The number of surviving seedlings from Plots A and B were almost identical. What can that mean? Well, Plot A was supposed to be the fungi-rich plot, whereas Plot B (the control) was supposed to be the fungi-normal plot. But here they have the same results (but notice that we're not told what those results are; it could be that no seedlings survived in any plots this time around.)

The question is phrased so that the three wrong choices are things that could explain the results; the correct choice will be the one that can't. Choices B, C, and D all can explain the results, since they all show how similar results could have been derived from Plots A and B. If the new soil just couldn't support life—fungi or no fungi—Plots A and B would have produced similar results, namely, no seedlings surviving. On the other end of the spectrum, choices C and

D show how the two plots might have produced similar high survival rates. If there were many myco fungi naturally in this soil (that's choice D), then there wouldn't be all that much difference between the soils in Plots A and B. And if the soil were naturally extremely fertile (that's choice C), there might be perfect survival rates no matter what the fungi situation. So all three of these answers would help to explain similar results in Plots A and B.

Choice A, however, wouldn't help, since it talks about the sterilized soil that's in Plot C. The soil in Plot C won't affect the results in Plots A and B, so choice A is the answer here—the factor that doesn't help to explain the results.

Study 2

This study takes the surviving seedlings from Plots A and B in Study 1 and just tests how much potassium (K) and phosphorus (P) the roots have used. The results are listed in the second and third columns of the table. (Notice the N/A—not applicable—for Plot C in these columns, since there were no surviving seedlings to test in Plot C!) The data show much better utilization of both substances in the Plot-A seedlings, the seedlings that grew in a fungi-rich soil. This data would tend to support a theory that the myco fungi aid in the utilization of K and P, and that this in turn aids survival in pine seedlings.

The only question that hinges on Study 2 is Question 5. It asks what generalization would be supported by the specific results of Study 2. Well, notice that Study 2 involved only measuring K and P. It did not involve survival rates (that was Study 1), so Choice A can't be right. And neither study measured growth rates, so B is out. As for

C, the minerals K and P were in the control group's soil, which was natural, untreated pine forest soil, so the results in choice C are clearly unsupported.

But the data *did* show that not all of the potassium (K) could be absorbed by pine seedlings. Only 18 percent was absorbed in Plot A, while only 10 percent was absorbed in Plot B. That's a long way from 100 percent, so choice D seems a safe generalization to make.

Of course, not all experiments on the ACT Science Reasoning subject test are specific-to-general experiments; some are general-to-specific procedures, with scientists making specific predictions based on accepted general premises. But the same kind of strict thinking—manipulating factors to narrow down possibilities—can get you points, no matter in what direction your thinking goes.

STEP 14:
CLASSIC SCIENCE STRATEGIES

On every Science Reasoning subject test you'll find one "Conflicting Viewpoints" passage, in which two scientists propose different theories about a particular scientific phenomenon. Often, the two theories are just differing interpretations of the same data. Other times, each scientist offers his own data to support his own opinion. In either case, it's essential that you know more or less what theory each scientist is proposing, and that you pay careful attention to how and where their theories differ.

In the second Science Reasoning step, we talked about how scientists think, and you should bring all of that learning to bear on the Conflicting Viewpoints passage. Since the scientists are disagreeing on interpretation, it's usually the case that they're engaging in specific-to-general thinking. They're each using specific data, sometimes the same specific data, but they're coming to very different general conclusions.

It's important to remember that your job is not to figure out which scientist is right and which is wrong. Instead, you'll be tested on whether you understand each scientist's position and the thinking behind it. That's what the questions will hinge on.

DON'T WASTE TIME TRYING TO FIGURE OUT WHICH SCIEN-
TIST IS "RIGHT." JUST WORRY ABOUT UNDERSTANDING THEIR
DIFFERENT VIEWPOINTS.

PREREADING THE CONFLICTING
VIEWPOINTS PASSAGE

When tackling the Conflicting Viewpoints passage, you'll probably
want to spend a little more time than usual on the prereading step
of the three-step method. On other Science Reasoning passages, as
we saw, your goal in prereading is to get a general idea of what's
going on, so that you can focus when you do the questions. But we
find that it pays to spend a little extra time with the Conflicting
Viewpoints passage in order to get a clearer idea of the opposing
theories and the data behind them.

REMEMBER: The three-step method goes like this:
* *Preread the passage.*
* *Consider the question stem.*
* *Refer to the passage (before looking at the choices).*

The passage will usually consist of a short introduction laying out
the scientific issue in question, followed by two different viewpoints
on that issue. Sometimes these viewpoints are presented under the
headings Scientist 1 and Scientist 2, or the headings might be
Theory 1 and Theory 2, Hypothesis 1 and Hypothesis 2, or something similar.

A scientific viewpoint on the ACT usually consists of two parts:

* A statement of the general theory
* A summary of the data behind the theory

Usually, the very first line of each viewpoint expresses the general
theory. So, for instance, Scientist 1's first sentence might be something like, "The universe will continue to expand indefinitely."

That's Scientist 1's viewpoint boiled down to a single statement. Scientist 2's first sentence might then be, "The forces of gravity will eventually force the universe to stop expanding and to begin contracting." That's Scientist 2's viewpoint, and it is clearly in direct contradiction to Scientist 1's.

> **DON'T PANIC IF YOU DON'T UNDERSTAND BOTH SCIENTISTS' POSITIONS. MANY QUESTIONS WILL HINGE ON JUST ONE OF THE SCIENTIST'S ARGUMENTS.**

It's very important that you understand these basic statements of theory, and, just as important, that you see how they're opposed to each other. In fact, you might want to circle the theory statement for each viewpoint, right there in the test booklet, to fix the two positions in your mind.

After each statement of theory will come the data that's behind it. As we said, sometimes the scientists are just drawing different interpretations from the same data. But usually, each will have different supporting data. There are two different kinds of data:

- Data that support the scientist's own theory
- Data that weaken the opposing scientist's theory

It's normally a good idea to identify the major points of data for each theory. You might underline a phrase or sentence that crystallizes each, or even take note of whether it primarily supports the scientist's own theory or shoots holes in the opposing theory.

Once you understand each scientist's theory and the data behind it, you'll be ready to move on to the questions. Remember that some of the questions will refer to only one of the viewpoints. Whatever you do, *don't mix up the two viewpoints!* A question asking about, for example, the data supporting Theory 2 may have wrong answers that perfectly describe the data for Theory 1. If you're careless, you can easily fall for one of these wrong answers.

> **ALWAYS DOUBLE-CHECK TO MAKE SURE YOU HAVEN'T ASSIGNED SCIENTIST 1'S IDEAS TO SCIENTIST 2, AND VICE VERSA.**

THE REAL THING

What follows is a full-fledged ACT-style Conflicting Viewpoints passage. Take six minutes or so to do the passage and all seven questions.

Passage III

Tektites are natural, glassy objects that range in size from the diameter of a grain of sand to that of a human fist. They are found in only a few well-defined areas, called *strewn fields*. Two theories about the origin of tektites are presented below.

Scientist 1:

Tektites almost certainly are extraterrestrial, probably lunar, in origin. Their forms show the characteristics of air-friction melting. In one study, flanged, "flying saucer" shapes similar to those of australites (a common tektite form) were produced by ablating lenses of tektite glass in a heated airstream that simulated atmospheric entry.

Atmospheric forces also make terrestrial origin extremely improbable. Aerodynamic studies have shown that because of atmospheric density, tektite-like material ejected from Earth's surface would never attain a velocity much higher than that of the surrounding air, and therefore would not be shaped by atmospheric friction. Most likely, tektites were formed either from meteorites or from lunar material ejected in volcanic eruptions.

Analysis of specimen #14425 from the *Apollo 12* lunar mission shows that the sample strongly resembles some of the tektites from the Australasian strewn field. Also tektites contain only a small fraction of the water that is locked into the structure of terrestrial volcanic glass. And tektites never contain unmelted crystalline material; the otherwise similar terrestrial glass produced by some meteorite impacts always does.

Scientist 2:

Nonlocal origin is extremely unlikely, given the narrow distribution of tektite strewn fields. Even if a tightly focused jet of lunar matter were to strike Earth, whatever was deflected by the atmosphere would remain in a solar orbit. The next time its orbit coincided with that of Earth, some of the matter would be captured by Earth's gravity and fall over a wide area.

There are striking similarities, not only between the composition of Earth's crust and that of most tektites, but between the proportions of various gases found in Earth's atmosphere and in the vesicles of certain tektites.

Tektites were probably formed by meteorite impacts. The shock wave produced by a major collision could temporarily displace the atmosphere above. Terrestrial material might then splatter to suborbital heights and undergo air-friction melting upon reentry. And tektite fields in the Ivory Coast and Ghana can be correlated with known impact craters.

Part Five: The ACT Science Reasoning Test

1. The discovery that many tektites contain unmelted, crystalline material would:

   A. tend to weaken Scientist 1's argument.

   B. tend to weaken Scientist 2's argument.

   C. be incompatible with both scientists' views.

   D. be irrelevant to the controversy.

2. Which of the following is a reason given by Scientist 2 for believing that tektites originate on Earth?

   F. The density of Earth's atmosphere would prevent any similar lunar or extraterrestrial material from reaching Earth's surface.

   G. Tektites have a composition totally unlike that of any material ever brought back from the Moon.

   H. Extraterrestrial material could not have been as widely dispersed as tektites are.

   J. Material ejected from the moon or beyond would eventually have been much more widely distributed on Earth.

Step 14: Classic Science Strategies

3. Scientist 1 could best answer the point that some tektites have vesicles filled with gases in the same proportion as Earth's atmosphere by:

   A. countering that not all tektites have such gas-filled vesicles.

   B. demonstrating that molten material would be likely to trap some gases while falling through the terrestrial atmosphere.

   C. suggesting that those gases might occur in the same proportions in the moon's atmosphere.

   D. showing that similar vesicles, filled with these gases in the same proportions, are also found in some terrestrial volcanic glass.

4. How did Scientist 2 answer the argument that tektitelike material ejected from Earth could not reach a high enough velocity relative to the atmosphere to undergo air-friction melting?

   F. By asserting that a shock wave might cause a momentary change in atmosphere density, permitting subsequent aerodynamic heating.

   G. By pointing out that periodic meteorite impacts have caused gradual changes in atmospheric density over the eons.

   H. By attacking the validity of the aerodynamic studies cited by Scientist 1.

   J. By referring to the correlation between tektite fields and known impact craters in the Ivory Coast and Ghana.

5. The point of subjecting lenses of tektite glass to a heated airstream was to:

    A. determine their water content.

    B. see if gases became trapped in their vesicles.

    C. reproduce the effects of atmospheric entry.

    D. simulate the mechanism of meteorite formation.

6. Researchers could best counter the objections of Scientist 2 to Scientist 1's argument by:

    F. Discovering some phenomenon that would quickly remove tektite-sized objects from orbit

    G. Proving that most common tektite shapes can be produced by aerodynamic heating

    H. Confirming that active volcanoes once existed on the moon

    J. Mapping the locations of all known tektite fields and impact craters

7. Which of the following characteristics of tektites is LEAST consistent with the theory that tektites are of extraterrestrial origin?

    A. Low water content

    B. "Flying saucer" shapes

    C. Narrow distribution

    D. Absence of unmelted material

ANSWERS: 1. A, 2. J, 3. B, 4. F, 5. C, 6. F, 7. C

IDENTIFYING THE CONFLICT

Your prereading of the introduction should have revealed the issue at hand—namely, tektites, which are small glassy objects found in certain areas known as *strewn fields*. The conflict is about the *origin* of these objects; in other words, where did they come from?

Scientist 1's theory is expressed in his first sentence: "Tektites almost certainly are extraterrestrial, probably lunar, in origin." Put that into a form you can understand. Scientist 1 believes that tektites come from space, probably the moon. Scientist 2, on the other hand, has an opposing theory, also expressed in her first sentence: "Nonlocal origin is extremely unlikely." In other words, it's unlikely that tektites came from a nonlocal source. Instead, they probably came from a *local* source—right here on Earth. The conflict is clear. One says that tektites come from space; the other says they come from Earth itself. You might have even labeled the two positions "space origin" and "Earth origin."

But how do these scientists support their theories? Scientist 1 presents three points of data:
- Tektite shapes show characteristics of air-friction melting (supporting the theory of space origin).
- Atmospheric forces wouldn't be great enough to shape tektitelike material ejected from Earth's surface (weakening the theory of Earth origin).
- Tektites resemble moon rocks gathered by *Apollo 12* but not Earth rocks (strengthening the theory of space origin).

Scientist 2 also presents three points of data:
- Any matter coming from space would fall over a wide area instead of being concentrated in strewn fields (weakening the theory of space origin).

- There are striking similarities between tektites and the composition of Earth's crust (strengthening the theory of Earth origin).
- Meteorite impacts could create shock waves, explaining how terrestrial material could undergo air-friction melting (strengthening the theory of Earth origin by counteracting Scientist 1's first point).

Obviously, you wouldn't want to write out the supporting data for each theory the way we've done above. But it probably would be a good idea to underline the key phrases in the data descriptions ("air-friction melting," "*Apollo 12*," etcetera) and number them. What's important is that you have an idea of what data supports which theory. The questions will then force you to focus, once you get to them.

ATTACKING THE QUESTIONS

Now let's quickly attack the questions:

Question 1 asks how it would affect the scientists' arguments if it were discovered that many tektites contain unmelted crystalline material. Well, Scientist 1 says that tektites *never* contain unmelted crystalline material, and that the terrestrial glass produced by some meteorite impacts *always* does. Therefore, by showing a resemblance between tektites and Earth materials, this discovery would weaken Scientist 1's argument for extraterrestrial origin. Choice A is correct.

For question 2, you had to identify which answer choice was used by Scientist 2 to support the argument that tektites are terrestrial in origin. You should have been immediately drawn to choice J, which expresses what we've identified above as Scientist 2's first data point.

Notice how choice F is a piece of evidence that Scientist 1 cites—remember not to confuse the viewpoints! As for G, Scientist 2 says that tektites do resemble Earth materials, but never says that they *don't* resemble lunar materials. And choice H gets it backwards; Scientist 2 says that extraterrestrial material *would* be widely dispersed, and that the tektites are *not* widely dispersed.

COUNTERING EVIDENCE

For question 3, you need to find the best way for Scientist 1 to counter the point that some tektites have vesicles filled with gases in the same proportion as Earth's atmosphere. First, make sure you understand the meaning of that point. The idea that these gases must have been trapped in the vesicles—little holes—while the rock was actually being formed is being used by Scientist 2 to suggest that tektites are of terrestrial origin. Scientist 1 *could* say that not all tektites have such gas-filled vesicles (choice A) but that's not a great argument. If any reasonable number of them *do,* Scientist 1 would have to come up with an alternative explanation (Scientist 2 never claimed that *all* tektites contained these vesicles).

But if, as B suggests, Scientist 1 could demonstrate that molten material would be likely to trap some terrestrial gases while falling through Earth's atmosphere, that would explain how tektites might have come from beyond the Earth and still contain vesicles filled with Earthlike gases. Choice C is easy to eliminate if you know that the moon's atmosphere is extremely thin—almost nonexistent—and totally different in composition from Earth's atmosphere, so it doesn't make much sense to suggest that those gases might occur in the same proportions in the moon's atmosphere. Finally, since it's Scientist 2 who claims that tektites are terrestrial in origin, showing that similar gas-filled vesicles occur in some terrestrial volcanic glass (choice D) wouldn't help Scientist 1 at all.

In question 4, you're asked how Scientist 2 answered the argument that tektitelike material ejected from Earth could not reach a high-enough velocity to undergo air-friction melting. Well, that was Scientist 2's third data point. The shock wave produced by a major meteorite collision could momentarily displace the atmosphere right above the impact site—just move the air out of the way for a very brief time—and so when the splattered material reentered the atmosphere, it would undergo air-friction melting. That's basically what choice F says, so F is correct.

Question 5: Subjecting lenses of tektite glass to a heated airstream was mentioned toward the beginning of Scientist 1's argument. The point was to simulate the entry of extraterrestrial tektite material through Earth's atmosphere, and that's closest to choice C.

KEEPING YOUR SCIENTISTS STRAIGHT

Question 6 shows again why it pays to keep straight whose viewpoint is whose. You can't counter the objections of Scientist 2 to Scientist 1's argument unless you know what Scientist 2 was objecting to. Scientist 2's first data point is the only one designed to shoot holes in the opposing viewpoint. There, Scientist 2 takes issue with the idea that lunar material could strike Earth without being dispersed over a far wider area than the known strewn fields. But if, as correct choice F says, researchers found some force capable of removing tektite-sized objects from orbit *quickly,* it would demolish the objection that Scientist 2 raises in her first paragraph. The tektite material would strike Earth or be pulled away quickly instead of remaining in a solar orbit long enough to get captured by Earth's gravity and subsequently get distributed over a wide area of Earth.

Question 7 wasn't too tough if you read the question stem carefully. You want to find the tektite characteristic that is *least* consistent with the theory that tektites came from the moon or beyond. That's Scientist 1's theory, so you want to pick the answer choice that doesn't go with his argument. Scientist 1's evidence *does* include tektites' low water content, "flying saucer" shapes, and absence of unmelted material. The only answer choice that he didn't mention was the narrow distribution of the strewn fields. And with good reason. That's part of Scientist 2's argument *against* an extraterrestrial origin. So the correct answer is choice C.

> **ALWAYS BE CAREFUL TO TAKE NOTE OF THE EVIDENCE (DATA)**
> **EACH SCIENTIST USES.**

WHAT TO DO WHEN YOU'RE RUNNING OUT OF TIME

Let's conclude now with another quick point about getting quick points. If you're nearly out of time and you still have a whole Science Reasoning passage left, you need to shift to last-minute strategies. *Don't* try to preread the passage, or you'll just run out of time before you answer any questions. Instead, scan the questions *without reading the passage* and look first for the ones that require only reading data off of a graph or table. You can often get a couple of quick points just by knowing how to find data quickly.

> **WHEN YOU'RE RUNNING OUT OF TIME, GO RIGHT TO THE**
> **QUESTIONS WITHOUT READING THE PASSAGE AND DO AS**
> **MANY DATA INTERPRETATION QUESTIONS AS YOU CAN.**

Again, the most important thing is to make sure you have gridded in at least a random guess on every question.

APPENDIX

LAST-MINUTE TIPS

Is it starting to feel like your whole life is a buildup to the ACT? You've known about it for years, you've worried about it for months, and now you've spent at least a few hours in solid preparation for it. As the test gets closer, you may find your anxiety is on the rise. But you really shouldn't worry. After the preparation you've received from this book, you're in good shape for Test Day.

To calm any pretest jitters you may have (and assuming you've left yourself at least some breathing time before your ACT), let's go over a few last-minute strategies for the couple of days before and after the test.

THREE DAYS BEFORE THE TEST

If you've left yourself enough time, take a full-length practice test under timed conditions. This can be an actual ACT or one of the practice tests contained in Kaplan's other ACT books.

Try to use all of the techniques and tips you've learned in this book. Take control. Approach the test strategically and creatively.

> *WARNING: Don't take a full practice ACT unless you have at least 48 hours left before the test! Doing so will probably exhaust you, hurting your scoring potential on the actual test! You wouldn't run a marathon the day before the real thing, would you?*

Appendix

TWO DAYS BEFORE THE TEST

Go over the results of your practice test. Don't worry too much about your score or whether you got a specific question right or wrong. Remember the practice test doesn't count. But do examine your performance on specific questions with an eye to how you might get through each one faster and with greater accuracy on the actual test to come.

After reviewing the results of your practice test, see what your "problem areas" are. Go back to the relevant sections of this book and study the techniques and strategies that will help you succeed in those areas on Test Day.

This is the day to do your last studying—review a couple of the more difficult principles we've covered, do a few more practice problems, and call it quits. It doesn't pay to make yourself crazy right before the test. Besides, you've prepared. You'll do well.

THE NIGHT BEFORE THE TEST

Don't study!

Get together an "ACT survival kit" containing the following items:
- A watch
- At least three sharpened No. 2 pencils
- A pencil sharpener
- Two erasers
- Photo ID card
- Your admission ticket
- A snack—there's a break, and you'll probably get hungry

Know exactly where you're going and how you're getting there. It's probably a good idea to visit your test center sometime before Test Day, so that you know what expect on the big day.

Read a good book, take a bubble bath, watch TV. Exercise can be a good idea early in the afternoon. Working out makes it easier to sleep when you're nervous, and it also makes many people feel better. Of course, don't work so hard that you can't get up the next day!

DON'T STUDY THE NIGHT BEFORE THE TEST. RELAX!

Get a good night's sleep. Go to bed early and allow for some extra time to get ready in the morning.

THE MORNING OF THE TEST

- Dress in layers so that you can adjust to the temperature of the test room.
- Eat breakfast. Make it something substantial, but not anything too heavy or greasy. Don't drink a lot of coffee if you're not used to it; bathroom breaks cut into your time, and too much caffeine—or any other kind of drug—is a bad idea.
- Read something. Warm up your brain with a newspaper or a magazine. Don't let the ACT be the first thing you read that day.
- Be sure to get there early. Allow yourself extra time for traffic, mass-transit delays, and any other possible problems. If you can, go to the test with a friend (even if he or she isn't taking the test). It's nice to have somebody supporting you right up to the last minute.

DURING THE TEST

Don't get rattled. If you find your confidence slipping, remind yourself that you know the test; you know the strategies; you know the material tested. You're in great shape, as long as you relax!

Appendix

Even if something goes really wrong, don't panic. If the test booklet is defective—two pages are stuck together or the ink has run—try to stay calm. Raise your hand, and tell the proctor you need a new book. If you accidentally misgrid your answer page or put the answers in the wrong section, again don't panic. Raise your hand, and tell the proctor. He or she might be able to arrange for you to re-grid your test after it's over, when it won't cost you any time.

AFTER THE TEST

Once the test is over, put it out of your mind. If you don't plan to take the ACT again, shelve this book and start thinking about more interesting things.

You might walk out of the ACT thinking that you blew it. This is a normal reaction. Lots of people—even the highest scorers—feel that way. You tend to remember the questions that stumped you, not the many that you knew.

If you really did blow the test, you can take it again and no admissions officer will be the wiser. Odds are, though, you didn't really blow it. Most people only remember their disasters on the test; they don't remember the numerous small victories that kept piling up the points. And no test experience is going to be perfect. If you were distracted by the proctor's hacking cough this time around, next time you may be even more distracted by construction noise, or a cold, or the hideous lime-green sweater of the person sitting in front of you.

DON'T CANCEL YOUR SCORE UNLESS YOU HAVE A GOOD, SOLID REASON. BUT IF YOU HAVE A GOOD REASON, DO IT.

KAPLAN

STRESS MANAGEMENT

The countdown has begun. Your date with THE TEST is looming on the horizon. Anxiety is on the rise. Butterflies in your stomach have gone ballistic. Perhaps you feel as if the last thing you ate has turned into a lead ball. Your thinking is getting cloudy. Maybe you think you won't be ready. Maybe you already know your stuff, but you're going into panic mode anyway. Worst of all, you're not sure of what to do about it.

Don't worry! It is possible to tame that anxiety and stress—before and during the ACT or any other test. We'll show you how. You won't believe how quickly and easily you can deal with that killer anxiety.

MAKING THE MOST OF YOUR PREP TIME

Lack of control is one of the prime causes of stress. A ton of research shows that if you don't have a sense of control over what's happening in your life you can easily end up feeling helpless and hopeless. So, just having concrete things to do and to think about—taking control—will help reduce your stress. This section shows you how to take control during the days leading up to the test.

IDENTIFY THE SOURCES OF STRESS

In the space provided, jot down anything you identify as a source of your test-related stress. The idea is to pin down that free-floating anxiety so that you can take control of it. Here are some common examples to get you started.

- I always freeze up on tests.
- I'm nervous about the math (or the grammar or reading comp, etcetera).
- I need a good/great score to go to Acme University.
- My older brother/sister/best friend/girl- or boyfriend did really well. I must match their scores or do better.
- My parents, who are paying for school, will be really disappointed if I don't test well.
- I'm afraid of losing my focus and concentration.
- I'm afraid I'm not spending enough time preparing.
- I study like crazy but nothing seems to stick in my mind.
- I always run out of time and get panicky.
- I feel as though thinking is becoming like wading through thick mud.

Sources of Stress

_____

_____

_____

_____

_____

_____

_____

_____

_____

_____

Take a few minutes to think about the things you've just written down. Then put them in some sort of order. List the statements you most associate with your stress and anxiety first, and put the least disturbing items last. Chances are, the top of the list is a fairly accurate description of exactly how you react to test anxiety, both physically and mentally. The later items usually describe your fears (disappointing mom and dad, looking bad, etcetera). As you write the list, you're forming a hierarchy of items so you can deal first with the anxiety-provokers that bug you most. Very often, taking care of the major items from the top of the list goes a long way towards relieving overall testing anxiety. You probably won't have to bother with the stuff you placed last.

TAKE STOCK OF YOUR STRENGTHS AND WEAKNESSES

Take one minute to list the areas of the ACT or any other test that you are good at. They can be general ("world history") or specific ("Nevada from 1850 to 1875"). Put down as many as you can think of, and if possible, time yourself. Write for the entire time; don't stop writing until you've reached the one-minute stopping point.

Appendix

Strong Test Subjects

_____

_____

_____

_____

_____

_____

Next, take one minute to list areas of the test you're not so good at, just plain bad at, have failed at, or keep failing at. Again, keep it to one minute, and continue writing until you reach the cutoff. Don't be afraid to identify and write down your weak spots! In all probability, as you do both lists you'll find you are strong in some areas and not so strong in others. Taking stock of your assets and liabilities lets you know the areas you don't have to worry about, and the ones that will demand extra attention and effort.

Weak Test Subjects

_____

_____

_____

_____

_____

_____

KAPLAN

Facing your weak spots gives you some distinct advantages. It helps a lot to find out where you need to spend extra effort. Increased exposure to tough material makes it more familiar and less intimidating. (After all, we mostly fear what we don't know and are probably afraid to face.) You'll feel better about yourself because you're dealing directly with areas of the test that bring on your anxiety. You can't help feeling more confident when you know you're actively strengthening your chances of earning a higher overall score.

Now, go back to the "good" list, and expand it for two minutes. Take the general items on that first list and make them more specific; take the specific items and expand them into more general conclusions. Naturally, if anything new comes to mind jot it down. Focus all of your attention and effort on your strengths. Don't underestimate yourself or your abilities. Give yourself full credit. At the same time, don't list strengths you don't really have; you'll only be fooling yourself.

Expanding from general to specific might go as follows. If you listed "world history" as a broad topic you feel strong in, you would then narrow your focus to include areas of this subject about which you are particularly knowledgeable. Your areas of strength might include modern European history, the events leading up to World War I, the Bolshevik revolution, etcetera.

Whatever you know comfortably (that is, almost as well as you know the back of your hand) goes on your "good" list. Okay. You've got the picture. Now, get ready, check your starting time, and start writing down items on your expanded "good" list.

Appendix

Strong Test Subjects: An Expanded List

_____

_____

_____

_____

_____

After you've stopped, check your time. Did you find yourself going beyond the two minutes allotted? Did you write down more things than you thought you knew? Is it possible you know more than you've given yourself credit for? Could that mean you've found a number of areas in which you feel strong?

You just took an active step towards helping yourself. Notice any increased feelings of confidence? Enjoy them.

Here's another way to think about your writing exercise. Every area of strength and confidence you can identify is much like having a reserve of solid gold at Fort Knox. You'll be able to draw on your reserves as you need them, and you can use your reserves to solve difficult questions, maintain confidence, and keep test stress and anxiety at a distance. The encouraging thing is that every time you recognize another area of strength, succeed at coming up with a solution, or get a good score on a test, you increase your reserves. And, there is absolutely no limit to how much self-confidence you can have or how good you can feel about yourself.

IMAGINE YOURSELF SUCCEEDING

This next little group of exercises is both physical and mental. It's a natural follow-up to what you've just accomplished with your lists.

First, get yourself into a comfortable sitting position in a quiet setting. Wear loose clothes. If you wear glasses, take them off. Then, close your eyes and breathe in a deep, satisfying breath of air. Really fill your lungs until your rib cage is fully expanded and you can't take in any more. Then, exhale the air completely. Imagine you're blowing out a candle with your last little puff of air. Do this two or three more times, filling your lungs to their maximum and emptying them totally. Keep your eyes closed, comfortably but not tightly. Let your body sink deeper into the chair as you become even more comfortable.

> STRATEGY: Forcing relaxation is like asking yourself to flap your arms and fly. You can't do it, and every push and prod only gets you more frustrated. Relaxation is something you don't work at. You simply let it happen. Think about it. When was the last time you tried to force yourself to go to sleep, and it worked?

With your eyes shut you can notice something very interesting. You're no longer dealing with the worrisome stuff going on in the world outside of you. Now you can concentrate on what happens *inside* you. The more you recognize your own physical reactions to stress and anxiety, the more you can do about them. You may not realize it, but you've begun to regain a sense of being in control.

Let images begin to form on the "viewing screens" on the back of your eyelids. You're experiencing visualizations from the place in your mind that makes pictures. Allow the images to come easily and naturally; don't force them. Imagine yourself in a relaxing situation. It might be in a special place you've visited before or one you've read about. It can be a fictional location that you create in your imagination, but a real-life memory of a place or situation you know is usually better. Make it as detailed as possible and notice as much as you can.

Stay focused on the images as you sink farther back into your chair. Breathe easily and naturally. You might have the sensations of any stress or tension draining from your muscles and flowing downward, out your feet and away from you.

Take a moment to check how you're feeling. Notice how comfortable you've become. Imagine how much easier it would be if you could take the test feeling this relaxed and in this state of ease. You've coupled the images of your special place with sensations of comfort and relaxation. You've also found a way to become relaxed simply by visualizing your own safe, special place.

Now, close your eyes and start remembering a real-life situation in which you did well on a test. If you can't come up with one, remember a situation in which you did something (academic or otherwise) that you were really proud of—a genuine accomplishment. Make the memory as detailed as possible. Think about the sights, the sounds, the smells, even the tastes associated with this experience. Remember how confident you felt as you accomplished your goal. Now start thinking about the upcoming test. Keep your thoughts and feelings in line with that prior, successful experience. Don't make comparisons between them. Just imagine taking the upcoming test with the same feelings of confidence and relaxed control.

This exercise is a great way to bring the test down to earth. You should practice this exercise often, especially when the prospect of taking the exam starts to bum you out. The more you practice it, the more effective the exercise will be for you.

Stress Management

EXERCISE YOUR FRUSTRATIONS AWAY

Whether it is jogging, walking, biking, mild aerobics, pushups, or a pickup basketball game, physical exercise is a very effective way to stimulate both your mind and body and to improve your ability to think and concentrate. A surprising number of students get out of the habit of regular exercise, ironically because they're spending so much time prepping for the exam. Also, sedentary people—this is medical fact—get less oxygen to the blood and hence to the head than active people. You can live fine with a little less oxygen; you just can't think as well.

Any big test is a bit like a race. Thinking clearly at the end is just as important as having a quick mind early on. If you can't sustain your energy level in the last sections of the exam, there's too good a chance you could blow it. You need a fit body that can weather the demands any big exam puts on you. Along with a good diet and adequate sleep, exercise is an important part of keeping yourself in fighting shape and thinking clearly for the long haul.

There's another thing that happens when students don't make exercise an integral part of their test preparation. Like any organism in nature, you operate best if all your "energy systems" are in balance. Studying uses a lot of energy, but it's all mental. When you take a study break, do something active instead of raiding the fridge or vegging-out in front of the TV. Take a 5- to 10-minute activity break for every 50 or 60 minutes that you study. The physical exertion gets your body into the act which helps to keep your mind and body in sync. Then, when you finish studying for the night and hit the sack you won't lie there, tense and unable to sleep, because your head is overtired and your body wants to pump iron or run a marathon.

One warning about exercise, however: It's not a good idea to exercise vigorously right before you go to bed. This could easily cause

KAPLAN 231

sleep onset problems. For the same reason, it's also not a good idea to study right up to bedtime. Make time for a "buffer period" before you go to bed: For 30 to 60 minutes, just take a hot shower, meditate, simply veg out.

THE DANGERS OF DRUGS

Using drugs (prescription or recreational) specifically to prepare for and take a big test is definitely self-defeating. (And if they're illegal drugs, you can end up with a bigger problem than the ACT on your hands.) Except for the drugs that occur naturally in your brain, every drug has major drawbacks—and a false sense of security is one of them.

Let's say while studying you find yourself getting tired, and you pop some kind of upper to stay alert. You're just wasting your time. Amphetamines make it hard to retain information. Mild stimulants, such as coffee, cola, or over-the-counter caffeine pills can sometimes help as you study, since they keep you alert. On the down side, they can also lead to agitation, restlessness, and insomnia. Some people can drink a pot of high-octane coffee and sleep like a baby. Others have one cup and start to vibrate. It all depends on your tolerance for caffeine. Remember, a little anxiety is a good thing. The adrenaline that gets pumped into your bloodstream helps you stay alert and think more clearly. But, too much anxiety and you can't think straight at all.

To reduce stress you should eat fruits and vegetables (raw is best, or just lightly steamed or nuked), low-fat protein such as fish, skinless poultry, beans, and legumes (like lentils), or whole grains such as brown rice, whole wheat bread and pastas (no bleached flour). Don't eat refined sugar—sweet, high-fat snacks (simple carbohydrates like sugar make stress worse, and fatty foods lower your immunity) or salty foods (they can deplete potassium, which you need for nerve functions).

Instead, go for endorphins—the "natural morphine." Endorphins have no side effects and they're free—you've already got them in your brain. It just takes some exercise to release them. Running around on the basketball court, bicycling, swimming, aerobics, power walking—these activities, cause endorphins to occupy certain spots in your brain's neural synapses. In addition, exercise develops staying power and increases the oxygen transfer to your brain. Go into the test naturally.

TAKE A DEEP BREATH . . .

Here's another natural route to relaxation and invigoration. It's a classic isometric exercise that you can do whenever you get stressed out—just before the test begins, even *during* the test. It's very simple and takes just a few minutes.

Close your eyes. Starting with your eyes and—without holding your breath—gradually tighten every muscle in your body (but not to the point of pain) in the following sequence:

1. Close your eyes tightly.
2. Squeeze your nose and mouth together so that your whole face is scrunched up. (If it makes you self-conscious to do this in the test room, skip the face-scrunching part.)
3. Pull your chin into your chest, and pull your shoulders together.
4. Tighten your arms to your body, then clench your fists.
5. Pull in your stomach.
6. Squeeze your thighs and buttocks together, and tighten your calves.

Appendix

7. Stretch your feet, then curl your toes (watch out for cramping in this part).

At this point, every muscle should be tightened. Now, relax your body, one part at a time, *in reverse order*, starting with your toes. Let the tension drop out of each muscle. The entire process might take five minutes from start to finish (maybe a couple of minutes during the test). This clenching and unclenching exercise should help you to feel very relaxed.

. . . AND KEEP BREATHING

Conscious attention to breathing is an excellent way of managing that ACT test stress (or any stress, for that matter). The majority of people who get into trouble during tests take shallow breaths. They breathe using only their upper chests and shoulder muscles, and may even hold their breath for long periods of time. Conversely, the test taker who by accident or design keeps breathing normally and rhythmically is likely to be more relaxed and in better control during the entire test experience.

So, now is the time to get into the habit of relaxed breathing. Do the next exercise to learn to breathe in a natural, easy rhythm. By the way, this is another technique you can use during the test to collect your thoughts and ward off excess stress. The entire exercise should take no more than three to five minutes.

With your eyes still closed, breathe in slowly and deeply through your nose. Hold the breath for a bit, and then release it through your mouth. The key is to breathe slowly and deeply by using your diaphragm (the big band of muscle that spans your body just above your waist) to draw air in and out naturally and effortlessly. Breathing with your diaphragm encourages relaxation and helps minimize tension. Try it and notice how relaxed and comfortable you feel.

QUICK TIPS FOR THE DAYS JUST BEFORE THE EXAM

- The best test takers do less and less as exam day approaches. Taper off on your study schedule and take it easy on yourself. You want to be relaxed and ready on test day. Give yourself time off, especially the evening before the exam. By that time, if you've studied well, everything you need to know is firmly stored in your memory banks.

- Positive self-talk can be extremely liberating and invigorating, especially as the test looms closer. Tell yourself things such as, "I *choose* to take this test" rather than "I *have* to"; "I *will* do well" rather than "I *hope* things go well"; "I *can*" rather than, "I *cannot*." Be aware of negative, self-defeating thoughts and images and immediately counter any you become aware of. Replace them with affirming statements that encourage your self-esteem and confidence. Create and practice doing visualizations that build on your positive statements.

- Get your act together sooner rather than later. Have everything (including choice of clothing) laid out days in advance. Most important, *know where the test will be held and the easiest, quickest way to get there.* You will gain great peace of mind if you know that all the little details—gas in the car, directions, etcetera—are firmly in your control before test day.

- Experience the test site a few days in advance. This is very helpful if you are especially anxious. If at all possible, find out what room your part of the alphabet is assigned to, and try to sit there (by yourself) for a while. Better yet, bring some practice material and do at least a section or two, if not an entire practice test, in that room. In this case, familiarity doesn't breed contempt, it generates comfort and confidence.

- Forego any practice on the day before the test. It's in your best interest to marshal your physical and psychological resources for 24 hours or so. Even race horses are kept in the paddock and treated like princes the day before a race. Keep the upcoming test out of your consciousness; go to a movie, take a pleasant hike, or just relax. Don't eat junk food or tons of sugar. And—of course—get plenty of rest the night before. Just don't go to bed too early. It's hard to fall asleep earlier than your used to, and you don't want to lie there thinking about the test.

- When you dress on test day, do it in loose layers. That way you'll be prepared no matter what the temperature of the room is. (An uncomfortable temperature will just distract you from the job at hand.) And, if you have an item of clothing that you tend to feel "lucky" or confident in—a shirt, a pair of jeans, whatever—wear it. A little totem couldn't hurt.

STRESS TIPS
- Don't work in a messy or cramped area. Before you sit down to study, clear yourself a nice, open space. And make sure you have books, paper, pencils—whatever tools you will need—within easy reach before you sit down to study.

- Don't study on your bed, especially if you have problems with insomnia. Your mind may start to associate the bed with work, and make it even harder for you to fall asleep.

- A lamp with a 75-watt bulb is optimal for studying. But don't keep it so close t that you create a glare.

- If you want to play music, keep it low and in the background. Music with a regular, mathematical rhythm—reggae, for example—aids the learning process. A recording of ocean waves is also soothing.

HANDLING STRESS DURING THE TEST

The biggest stress monster will be test day itself. Fear not; there are methods of quelling your stress during the test.

- Keep moving forward instead of getting bogged down in a difficult question. You don't have to get everything right to achieve a fine score. The best test takers skip difficult material in search of the easier stuff. They mark the ones that require extra time and thought. This strategy buys time and builds confidence so you can handle the tough stuff later.

- Don't be thrown if other test takers seem to be working more busily and furiously than you are. Continue to spend your time patiently but doggedly thinking through your answers; it's going to lead to better results. Don't mistake the other people's sheer activity for progress and higher scores.

- *Keep breathing!* Weak test takers forget to breathe properly as the test proceeds. They start holding their breath without realizing it, or they breathe erratically or arrhythmically. Improper breathing interferes with clear thinking.

- Some quick isometrics during the test—especially if concentration is wandering or energy is waning—can help. Try this: Put your palms together and press intensely for a few seconds. Concentrate on the tension you feel through your palms, wrists, forearms, and up into your biceps and shoulders. Then, quickly release the pressure. Feel the difference as you let go. Focus on the warm relaxation that floods through the muscles. Now you're ready to return to the task.

- Here's another isometric exercise that will relieve tension in both your neck and eye muscles. Slowly rotate your head from side to side, turning your head and eyes to look as far back over each shoulder as you can. Feel the muscles stretch on one side of your neck as they contract on the other. Repeat five times in each direction.

With what you've just learned here, you're armed and ready to do battle with the ACT—or any other test. This book and your studies will give you the information you'll need to answer the questions. It's all firmly planted in your mind. You also know how to deal with any excess tension that might come along, both when you're studying for and taking the exam. You've experienced everything you need to tame your test anxiety and stress. You *are* going to get a great score.

NOTES

NOTES

NOTES

NOTES

How Did We Do? Grade Us.

Thank you for choosing a Kaplan book. Your comments and suggestions are very useful to us. Please answer the following questions to assist us in our continued development of high-quality resources to meet your needs.

The title of the Kaplan book I read was: _____

My name is: _____

My address is: _____

_____

My e-mail address is: _____

What overall grade would you give this book?   Ⓐ   Ⓑ   Ⓒ   Ⓓ   Ⓕ

How relevant was the information to your goals?   Ⓐ   Ⓑ   Ⓒ   Ⓓ   Ⓕ

How comprehensive was the information in this book?   Ⓐ   Ⓑ   Ⓒ   Ⓓ   Ⓕ

How accurate was the information in this book?   Ⓐ   Ⓑ   Ⓒ   Ⓓ   Ⓕ

How easy was the book to use?   Ⓐ   Ⓑ   Ⓒ   Ⓓ   Ⓕ

How appealing was the book's design?   Ⓐ   Ⓑ   Ⓒ   Ⓓ   Ⓕ

What were the book's strong points? _____

How could this book be improved? _____

Is there anything that we left out that you wanted to know more about?

Would you recommend this book to others?   ☐ YES   ☐ NO

Other comments: _____

_____

_____

Do we have permission to quote you?   ☐ YES   ☐ NO

Thank you for your help.
Please tear out this page and mail it to:

    Managing Editor
    Kaplan, Inc.
    888 Seventh Avenue
    New York, NY 10106

Thanks!

About Kaplan

KAPLAN TEST PREPARATION & ADMISSIONS

With 3,000 classroom locations throughout the U.S. and abroad, Kaplan has served more than three million students in its classes over the past 60-plus years. Kaplan's nationally-recognized programs for roughly 35 standardized tests include entrance exams for secondary school, college and graduate school as well as English language and professional licensing exams. Kaplan also offers private tutoring and one-on-one admissions guidance and is a leader in test prep for computerized exams. Kaplan is the first major player to provide online test prep to students across the globe, as well as admissions courses and other resources at **www.kaptest.com**.

SCORE! LEARNING, INC.

SCORE! Learning, Inc. is a national provider of customized learning programs for students. SCORE! Educational Centers help students in K-10 build confidence along with academic skills in a motivating, sports-oriented environment after school and on weekends. SCORE! Prep provides in-home, one-on-one tutoring for high school academic subjects and standardized tests. SCORE! Educational Centers and SCORE! Prep share a highly personalized approach, proven educational techniques, and the goal of cultivating a love of learning in children.

THE KAPLAN COLLEGES

The Kaplan Colleges system (**www.kaplancollege.edu**) is a collection of institutions offering an extensive array of online and traditional educational programs for working professionals who want to advance their careers. Learners will find programs leading to bachelor and associates degrees, certificates and diplomas in fields such as business, IT, paralegal studies, legal nurse consulting, criminal justice and financial planning. The Kaplan Colleges system includes Concord Law School (**www.concordlawschool.com**), the nation's only online law school, offering J.D., Executive J.D. and LL.M. degrees for working professionals, family caregivers, students in rural communities, and others whose circumstances prevent them from attending a fixed facility law school.

QUEST EDUCATION CORPORATION

Kaplan's Quest Education unit (**www.questeducation.com**) is a leading provider of post-secondary education. Quest offers bachelor and associate degrees and diploma programs designed to provide students with the skills necessary to qualify them for entry-level employment. Programs are primarily in the fields of healthcare, business, information technology, fashion and design.

KAPLAN PUBLISHING

Kaplan Publishing, in a joint venture with Simon & Schuster, publishes more than 150 titles on test preparation, admissions, education, career development, and life skills. Kaplan Publishing emerged as a leader in sales of books for statewide assessments with the publication of dozens of new state test titles. Books are offered in traditional paper form, pre-packaged with computer software, and now in e-book form.

KAPLAN INTERNATIONAL

Kaplan International (**www.kaptest.com**) provides students and professionals with intensive English instruction, university preparation, test preparation programs, housing and activities at 12 city and campus centers in the U.S. and Canada. Kaplan also has a strong presence overseas with 41 centers in 18 countries outside of the United States.

KAPLAN COMMUNITY OUTREACH

Kaplan Community Outreach provides educational resources and opportunities to thousands of economically disadvantaged students annually. Kaplan joins forces with numerous nonprofit groups, educational institutions, government agencies, and other grass-roots organizations on a variety of local and national support programs. These programs help students and professionals from a variety of backgrounds achieve their educational and career goals.

KAPLAN PROFESSIONAL

The Kaplan Professional companies (**www.kaplanprofessional.com**) provide licensing and continuing education, training, certification, professional development courses, and compliance tracking for securities, insurance, financial services, legal, IT, and real estate professionals and corporations. Offering an array of educational tools, from on-site training and classroom instruction to nearly 200 online courses and programs, Kaplan Professional serves professionals who must maintain licenses and comply with regulatory mandates despite busy travel schedules and work obligations.

■ **Dearborn Financial Services** provides innovative education and compliance solutions to the financial services industry, including registration services, firm element needs analysis and training plan development, securities and insurance prelicensing training, continuing education, and compliance management services, in classes nationwide, online and via books and software.

■ **Dearborn Trade Publishing** publishes approximately 250 titles specializing in finance, business management and real estate, plus well-read consumer real estate books to help homebuyers, sellers and real estate investors make informed decisions.

■ **Dearborn Real Estate Education** is the leading real estate content provider for real estate schools and associations, offering practical prelicensing and continuing education training materials on appraisal, home inspection, property management, brokerage, ethics, law, sales approaches, and contracts, and an online real estate campus at **RECampus.com**.

■ **Perfect Access Speer** is a leader in software education and consulting, bringing both traditional and e-learning solutions to its clients in the legal, financial, and professional services industries.

■ **The Schweser Study Program** offers training tools for the Chartered Financial Analyst (CFA®) examination, with a comprehensive product line of study notes, audiotapes, videotapes, flashcards and live seminars that are developed and taught by a top-notch faculty.

■ **Kaplan Professional Real Estate Schools** provide real estate licensing and continuing education programs through live classroom instruction, Internet-based learning, and correspondence courses, to help real estate professionals acquire the skills needed to meet state licensing and educational requirements.

■ **Self Test Software** is a world leader in exam simulation software and preparation for technical certifications including Microsoft, Oracle, Cisco, Novell, Lotus, CIW and CompTIA, serving businesses and individuals seeking to attain vendor-sponsored certification.

■ **Call Center Solutions** provides assessment and training services to the call center industry.